CREATING NEW CLIENTS
2nd Edition

Creating
New Clients
Selling professional services

Kevin Walker,
Cliff Ferguson and
Paul Denvir

2nd Edition

 PACE

Creating New Clients
2nd Edition

Published by The PACE Partners LLP
Copyright The PACE Partners LLP 2012

For more information, contact The PACE Partners LLP, PACE House, Churchfield Road, Walton on Thames, Surrey, KT12 2TZ or visit us at: http://www.thepacepartners.com

ISBN 0-9552273-1-3
ISBN 978-0-9552273-1-8
ISBN 978-0-9552273-4-9

First published 1998 by Continuum
Reprinted 1999, 2000, 2001 and 2002 by Continuum
Reprinted 2003, 2004 and 2005 by Thomson Learning
Reprinted 2006 by The PACE Partnership
2nd Edition first published 2012 by The PACE Partners LLP

Contents

Introduction to the 2nd Edition

Since this book was originally published we have continued to work with tens of thousands of professional fee earners and the book itself can be seen on the shelves of professional services firms of every type and size. We have learned new things over the years but we have also learned that the keys to success in selling professional services remain consistent. In updating this book we have kept the essential elements of best practice that were already there and added the most important new ideas that we have learned from working with a host of very bright people.

In the introduction to the original edition we explored the need for such a book and, it is clear, the need is still very much there. The world of professional services is changing at an accelerating rate. In the 'good old days' some professionals were able to build very successful careers in a buoyant economy by being excellent at their job and waiting for the phone to ring. This strategy is becoming less and less successful. For today's fee earner technical excellence is a necessary but not sufficient determinant of success; in many firms with which we work, fee earners today have to be more proactive than their predecessors to achieve the success they are aiming for.

We also observe that the overall quality of selling has improved in most firms and most sectors of the marketplace which means that, as standards improve, it takes even more skill and more focused effort to achieve the same level of success. It is unfortunately also true that we still see, on a regular basis, examples of professionals attempting to sell their expertise without the confidence and skills necessary for sustained success. Even the best we have seen are not perfect and it is usually those people who are forever looking for ways to get even better. This book is not intended to be remedial - we believe that any fee earner in any firm, however experienced and successful, will find the ideas and approaches of value.

The book remains focused on the specific challenges involved in selling professional services - as opposed to any other product or service - and is based on the belief that long term success has as its foundation trust and integrity and the development and maintenance of the 'right' reputation and enough of the 'right' long term relationships. The book remains practical rather than overly theoretical.

This edition of the book is focused solely on the skills needed to win high quality new clients. For many firms the priority is necessarily on keeping and developing existing client relationships and we have written another book, *Managing Key Clients*, which focuses on this. The major difference between this edition and the first is that we have taken out all of the detail originally included on the process of winning new clients (The PACE Pipeline). All of this detail is available and up to date in our third publication *Growing Your Client Base*. We have however kept one introductory chapter on the PACE Pipeline to provide a context for the new business skills with which this book deals. This chapter is an excerpt from the opening chapter of *Growing Your Client Base*.

One further observation. We are very often reminded of the difficulty of differentiating one firm from another and of developing the genuine USPs (Unique Selling Points/ Propositions) that in an ideal world would help a firm's or individual's expertise to 'sell itself'. While it should be a major focus of the firm to ensure that its services are as attractive as possible to its clients and potential clients and to search continuously for ways of building a competitive advantage, in our experience one of the best ways of achieving that advantage is through the - better and more consistent - application of the skills and practices in this book by as many people in the firm as possible.

We hope you find this new edition of *Creating New Clients* to be as much value as have the many individuals who have bought the book since it was first published.

Introduction

THE NEED FOR THIS BOOK

Most people study accountancy, law and engineering because they want to graduate into careers as accountants, lawyers and engineers. Very few professionals studied to enter their profession with the desire at the back of their minds to become salespeople. However, as individuals progress in their vocation the nature of work can change. Typically over time professionals become less involved in the technical aspects of doing the job and start to become involved in managing some of the work. Managing involves an interface with the client. This interface often includes the responsibility for the development of on-going work from the client. Further down the career path the responsibility can be extended to seeking new work for the firm. In effect the accountant, lawyer and engineering consultant have 'graduated' into a business development role.

With years of study and practice the tax specialist, architect or technology consultant builds knowledge and skills related to their area of expertise. They understand intimately the processes of their profession. When adopting the new role of business developer for the firm, the professional has to build new knowledge and skills and has to understand a different process. This book is written to help define the most productive selling processes, to build the knowledge of the professional and to clearly delineate the skills required for maximum success in marketing and selling the professional service firm.

Our experience shows us that there are a number of reasons why professionals have to create new clients. It may be because:

- There has been fee income attrition from the client base. The reasons for this may be within our control. For example, the last piece of work for a client could have been perceived to have provided poor value. On the other hand the attrition can be for reasons beyond our control; perhaps a takeover has meant that the acquiring organisation's advisers have taken our client

- The nature of some work is transactional and non-recurring - for instance much Corporate Finance work. This means there is a constant need to develop new clients

- The firm has ambitious growth targets and the best predictions of income from on-going and new work from current clients will not hit the target figure. New clients have to be found

- Firms decide to enter new markets they have never been involved in previously. By definition the client base is zero. The only way forward is to create new clients

- Promotion to senior positions in some firms is dependent on the professional being a proven business developer. This may mean that the professional has to demonstrate an ability to win new work from non-clients

We have met very few professionals who get involved in creating new clients because it is a first-choice activity for them. It is an activity which has to be carried out. Nonetheless the reasons driving the creation of new clients are compelling and the successful management of this process is vital to firms who seek to grow their business.

WHAT THIS BOOK IS AND ISN'T ABOUT

If someone asked us the smartest way to increase fee income next year we would not answer, 'Go out and create some new clients.' In most situations this would be poor advice. Our guidance would typically be as follows:

1. Get close to your existing clients and ensure that work which should be captive, is captive. Guarantee ownership of any recurring work.

2. Look for new opportunities within your existing clients to help them with your expertise. It is far easier, quicker and cheaper to sell to existing clients than to create new clients.

3. Encourage your existing clients to provide you with referrals and introductions to other parts of their organisation (where you do not currently get work) or to other prospective clients whom they know.

4. You need still more work? OK, go on and create new clients.

We could easily have chosen to write this book on subjects 1, 2 and 3. After all, for most firms over 90 per cent of next year's income will be derived from these sources. However, this book is exclusively focused on the fourth topic.

We have not selected this as the most important topic - clearly for most firms it cannot be. It must be more important to secure 90 per cent of the income, not 10 per cent. This fourth area, though, is seen by most people in professional firms as being the most difficult and the one which appears to be most foreign to their natural instincts. That is why this book is about creating new clients.

WHAT IS THE DIFFERENCE BETWEEN THIS BOOK AND ANY OTHER BOOK ON THE SUBJECT OF SELLING?

As the authors of this book we have spent over sixty years between us working in selling, sales management and marketing. We continue as practitioners of these skills within our own business. In the last ten years we have all spent a high proportion of our time working with professional firms - accountancy firms, lawyers, surveyors, specialist consultancies, consulting engineers, architects and so on.

What we have not tried to do is to shoehorn practices which sit comfortably in say, the FMCG (Fast Moving Consumer Goods) business, into the professional services market. There is a very big difference between selling a product and selling a business-to-business professional service. The buying and selling of professional services is special because:

• The professional is very often (literally) selling himself. Chemistry and trust are much more important factors in the decision to buy

• The decision to buy often involves a decision to confide business-critical information to a third party. Such buying decisions are not taken lightly

• The decision to buy from a professional services firm can mean a long-term commitment. Some professional services are short term and transactional but most are purchased with the intention of a long and on-going relationship

- The selling process in most professional firms is carried out by people whose primary role and training is in another field of expertise - their profession

- When the professional service is sold, the professional then has to put on a different hat and become the creator and provider of the service. (Imagine a computer salesman having to go back to the factory to assemble the computers he sold the day before!) This means that the marketing and selling of professional services can become sporadic. One cannot be out selling while assembling computers on the production line. This is a recognised constraint when selling professional services

The authors of this book recognise all of the above scenarios. They represent the starting point for us.

Having spent so much of our time working with engineering consultancies, actuaries, law firms, accountancy practices and consultants of all types, we know that these businesses are different from each other. However, we believe that, in many ways, the commonalities outweigh the differences.

This is implicitly recognised today by the growth of both national and regional organisations which aim to improve professional services marketing. They attract members from every corner of the professional market. For this reason we are confident that the content of this book has application and value to anyone who is selling their expertise in this highly competitive field.

WHY PROFESSIONALS ARE UNCOMFORTABLE WITH SELLING AND FACE-TO-FACE MARKETING ACTIVITIES

The image of selling and face-to-face marketing

For many professionals the image of selling sits poorly with their self-image.

Selling is often personified by the 'foot in the door' and 'I'll stay here until you sign' approach, which is associated (rightly or wrongly) with the archetypal double glazing salesperson.

Other images which spring easily to mind are the techniques of harassment and spurious incentives employed by timeshare merchants.

Stories of gullible people being sold unsuitable pensions and other financial products also reach the newspapers on a regular basis.

There is nothing wrong with buying double glazing or deciding that timeshare is an excellent way to organise holidays. Pensions and financial protection are excellent concepts. What is wrong is not the product or service - it is the intent with which the sellers approach their potential buyers. The products in themselves are totally amoral. It is the approach of the salespeople which reflects morality or immorality. Lying and putting people under pressure in order to sell them something is immoral whatever the product or service being sold. Putting one's personal well-being and the health of one's own organisation before the well-being of the client is poor selling - no matter who you are and what your organisation produces.

All products and services can be sold morally, if people have the integrity and values to approach the selling and buying process from an ethical standpoint. We have made every effort in this book to do just this in our approach to the selling of professional services. If you are looking for 'tricks' and short-cuts to get people to commit to your services when they don't really need them, please put this book down now.

If you want to know how to win new clients using totally professional and ethical methods, this book is for you. Good selling practice is totally consistent with ethical practice.

Professionals have a particular fear of failure

Professionals give advice. They spend their lives being paid to be right. This is the nature of most professional work. Professionals are not used to being wrong, and being wrong is anathema to them. In his Harvard Business Review article, 'Teaching Smart People How to Learn', Chris Argyris publishes his research conclusions on why professionals can find learning more difficult. Argyris says, 'People who rarely experience failure end up not knowing how to deal with it effectively.'

Essentially, if we are always used to being right we find it very difficult to accept that we can be wrong. The tendency is to defend our actions - not admit that we have erred in judgement.

Selling and marketing are not exact sciences and we will never make all of our efforts work perfectly all of the time. There is going to be failure. All selling and marketing is partially a 'numbers game'. Not every prospect becomes a client. Not every selling meeting identifies work opportunities. Not every proposal wins.

This reality can have two negative effects:

- Some professionals avoid selling and marketing work where the chances of failure are highest (and selling to win new clients is definitely in this category). Thereby they avoid the pain of failure

- Professionals are not open to examination of the way they have conducted a selling process to a client. Losing will be ascribed to either dirty tricks from competitors, stupid clients or uncontrollable factors. Any shortcomings in negotiating these hurdles will then be rationalised away. Many will not have their management of the selling process candidly examined and criticised. In this way they avoid the pain of failure

There is only one answer to this problem. When engaged in marketing and selling activities we have to discard the benchmarks which serve us well in assessing our professional performance. They are not relevant to assessing our performance in the processes of creating new clients. We are not suggesting accepting lower benchmarks - we are advocating totally different benchmarks. This is a different activity, a different process and different measures of performance are required.

OUR APPROACH

Practical, not theoretical

We have an intense interest in things which really work. Put another way, we are not interested in clever theory which will not stand the rigours of application in the field. This book is a real nuts and bolts 'How to' publication.

Much of what we have included has been learned through direct first-hand experience - selling our own capabilities and expertise. However, we are not averse to learning from others. We pick up ideas through our own reading, we learn from training and we learn from the experiences which our clients relate to us. What we have included in this book is the distillation of best practice we have accumulated in our careers to date.

Will we learn more? Will we improve and add to our ideas? We certainly hope so. This is intended to be an authoritative word on the subject - not the last word.

Examples and illustrations

In many places in the text we have given examples of dialogue. There are some points to bear in mind regarding these illustrations.

- These examples are given in order to bring the 'theory' to life

- They are probably not the words that you may choose to use

- We are not claiming that this is the only way the dialogue could develop

In all our training we stress that we are not trying to change people's personalities. What we are attempting to do is to encourage participants to apply certain skills and practices, using their own personality to project these. We would encourage readers likewise.

Gender distinctions

For simplicity we have decided to be politically incorrect. In all instances when we refer to the professional this person will be male. When we refer to the client this person will always be female. This saves a multiplicity of he/shes and his/hers.

References

The following works are referred to in the text:

'Teaching Smart People How to Learn' by Chris Argyris
(Harvard Business Review, May/June 1997).

Personal Selling Strategies for Consultants and Professionals by Richard Carlson
(John Wiley and Sons).

'How Clients Choose' by David Maister
(from Managing the Professional Service Firm, Free Press).

Marketing Warfare and Positioning by Al Ries and Jack Trout
(McGraw-Hill).

Section 1 The PACE Pipeline

Chapter 1 **Introducing The PACE Pipeline**

WHAT IS THE PACE PIPELINE?

The PACE Pipeline is a model that enables a firm to have a clear picture of its business development processes and practice. Adoption and application of The PACE Pipeline model brings certainty to a firm's business development efforts. Firms that use the model can plan more accurately the marketing and business development activities they need to carry out and can then analyse the effect of these plans in a structured way. A whole firm can adopt the model or specific practice areas or market facing groups within a firm can apply it. It can even be used by individual fee earners.

So, what is The PACE Pipeline?

The PACE Pipeline is a tool for the effective project management of business development in professional services firms

Professional firms today have, in the main, reasonable systems that tell them about the current financial health of the organisation. They know what they have billed, they know what work in progress is still to be billed and they know the work they have booked that they have yet to commence. Too often that is where the measurement and management of fee-earning work finishes. The systems measure the here and now but do nothing about reassuring (or warning) management about the health of future income streams.

The PACE Pipeline and pipeline management are all about ensuring that future fee income is both secure and profitable. In our parlance a practice area that has a strong pipeline would be very certain that future business flow (perhaps three, six or twelve months into the future) was going to be healthy because it had created opportunities that it would be able to convert into future work. People within the practice area - carrying out specific, planned and targeted activities with the firm's clients and prospective clients - have created these opportunities.

The PACE Pipeline is the foundation for the successful management of business development activities.

The model has particular relevance for business development scenarios where the following conditions are typical.

1. It is hard (or impossible) to guarantee the level of future sales (fee) income.

2. There is a time lag between activities put into business development and billable results being produced from this activity.

3. Not all business development activity produces results.

4. It is possible to measure (and manage) business development activity.

We would suggest that these criteria all apply in great measure to the selling of professional services.

On the first point it is a brave individual who guarantees the fee income he will produce next year. Sometimes it takes courage to take a stab at the fee income projection for next month!

Secondly there is certainly a time lag between activity put into business development (particularly new client acquisition) and the ensuing results. Non-clients have relationships with other people at other firms. It may take months or years to break these loyalty ties and win a first piece of work.

Related to the third point all professionals are only too aware that not every effort directed toward business development reaches a successful conclusion. As someone once expressed it to us, "You have to kiss a lot of frogs before you find a prince".

Finally business development activity can be measured. The fact that most firms have poor processes for doing so does not get us away from the fact that this activity can be measured. And what can be measured can be managed.

If a firm's pipeline building activities are well managed then it can be assured of the fee income streams that will guarantee a healthy future. To identify exactly what these activities are we should refer to the model.

The Segments of the Model

There are six parts to The PACE Pipeline model, five lying within the model and one outside. The five parts that lie within are known collectively as the Total Defined Market. Whether client or prospective client these parts of the pipeline are known and defined. Outside the model lie a firm's undefined prospects.

P0 - Undefined Prospects

Outside the perimeter of the model exists the overall market. Within this market there are thousands of organisations that potentially could become clients of the firm. Some we would welcome, some would be a poor fit.

P1 - Defined Prospects not yet marketed to

From the overall marketplace a firm has to make choices as to which prospective clients it would ideally like to work with in the future. Having initially made the choice, there may be a period of time before the firm begins its marketing and business development activities directed toward these organisations.

P2 - Defined Prospects marketed to - not yet in dialogue

Having identified its Defined Prospects a firm then has to begin the process of making the prospect aware of its existence and what it does. Ideally it also tries to convince the client that it is particularly adept in its particular field - perhaps better than the advisers they are using today. Marketing tools and activities are employed to achieve these aims.
The objective is to encourage the Defined Prospect to welcome the opportunity to discuss the possibility of working with the firm.

P3 - Qualified Prospects

Having created the opportunity to cross the threshold of the Defined Prospect's premises in order to talk business, some of these prospective clients will have a genuine opportunity that is within the remit and capabilities of the firm making the approach. When there is real opportunity that has been qualified as 'winnable' then our Defined Prospect has turned into a Qualified Prospect.

P4 - Current key and valued clients

The successful pursuit of an opportunity identified within a Qualified Prospect leads to the acquisition of a client. In the fullness of time this client may qualify to be recognised as one of the firm's key clients. If not a key client then the client is categorised as one of the firm's valued clients. The distinction between key clients and valued clients - and how a firm may decide how to segment its client base - is covered in some depth in our book *Managing Key Clients*.

P5 - 'Problem children' clients

Every firm has them. Some have more than others. Some have their client base largely built on 'problem children'. These are clients that, in their current state, probably cause the firm more grief than the fee income is worth.

Each of the segments of The PACE Pipeline has a title that reflects the main activity that is occurring at each stage of the pipeline building process - prospecting, promoting, projecting (that we will win work at some point in the future), protecting and (potentially) pruning.

Pipeline Building Activity

The arrows on The PACE Pipeline model represent the activities in which a firm has to engage in order to build its pipeline of future business. In sequence the activities are as follows.

Arrow 1

This is the work that has to be carried out in order that the firm can accurately identify those organisations in the marketplace that it wishes to do business with at some point in the future. Success in this activity produces a clearly agreed list of Defined Prospects. This list is compiled through the application of relevant selection criteria to prospective clients in the overall (P0) marketplace.

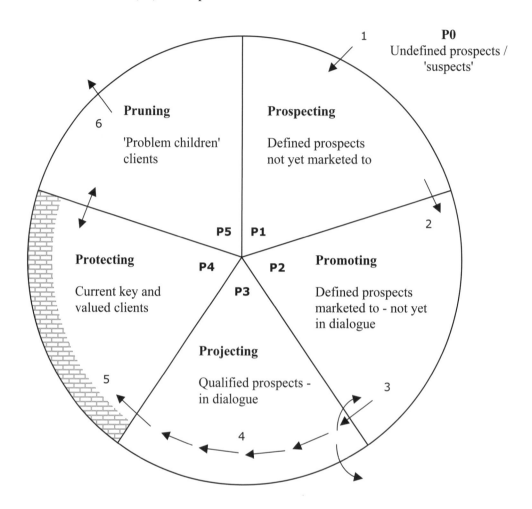

Arrow 2

This is the marketing activity that is directed toward Defined Prospects. There are a plethora of marketing tools and activities available to a professional services firm. It is critical that firms understand the potential effect of each of the marketing tools available and know how to apply them successfully.

Arrow(s) 3

The result of excellent marketing activity directed toward prospective clients is a ringing telephone - the Defined Prospect calling us and telling us that they would like to talk with someone from our firm. In an ideal world this would happen all the time. In the real world it only happens some of the time. When it doesn't happen then fee earners within the firm have to be prepared, when the timing is right, to pick up the telephone and make proactive verbal contact with people within the Defined Prospect organisation with a view to agreeing a meeting. This is *not* however about cold calling, it is about building this potential client's motivation to meet. It is vital that the people we want to meet *want* to meet with us, not feel forced, bullied or cajoled into a meeting. The strategies and approaches that achieve success here (and in all the other stages of the Pipeline building process) are detailed in our book *Growing Your Client Base*.

In the ideal world a first meeting with a Defined Prospect would always result in:

- Our image of the Defined Prospect as a desirable future client even more enhanced by the conclusion of the meeting

- The identification of a real opportunity that we are interested in pursuing and the client is interested in discussing further with us

Back in the real world neither of these ideal scenarios occur every time. Our cluster of arrows at action stage 3 shows three possibilities. The best outcome is the straight arrow. We proceed to the fourth set of arrows in the business development process.

However, in the course of an initial meeting we may uncover any number of facts that lead us to other conclusions. As much as the prospect may have looked interesting from our initial due diligence back at the arrow 1 stage, in fact there may be very good reasons why at this point we do not wish to pursue them any further. As shallow and superficial as it may sound, we have walked into reception areas of prospects and before we have started the first meeting we have recognised that the business whose representative we are due to meet with will probably not fit as one of our chosen clients. This interim conclusion is based on evidence that is visual and verbal. The following hour allows time for gathering more evidence on which to make a final decision. If, based on first-hand experience, the prospect is unsuitable we should not pursue the contact further but rather return the organisation back to the P0 'pool'.

More common is the arrow that returns the Defined Prospect to the P2 Promoting segment of the pipeline.

In this instance we finish the meeting still convinced that the Defined Prospect is the sort of organisation that we would like to have as a client someday, but with no specific opportunity having been agreed between the two parties that would provide the basis for immediate on-going dialogue. In this situation the Defined Prospect should then continue to be targeted through our marketing. The fact that we did not find an immediate opportunity at the first meeting does not mean that everything that went before was wrong. It simply means that our timing was out.

We have to ensure that when a potential opportunity does occur in the future that we are far enough to the front of the Defined Prospect's mind that they include us in their thinking. As Woody Allen said in one of his movies, "80% of success is showing up". We have to continue to 'show up' by using our marketing tools and by keeping in contact via e-mail, voicemail, the telephone and through the considered and skillful use of social media.

Professional firms in general are poor at maintaining this sort of on-going contact. Fee earners conclude that there is nothing much to be won from the prospective client and whilst there is an initial intention to keep in contact, this lapses quickly as the professional becomes engaged in other priorities - mostly fee-earning work. The real damage of this behaviour is only experienced some time - maybe months or years - later when a colleague contacts the prospective client again to hear: "I don't know why you're contacting us again. One of your people was here about a year ago. Made all sorts of promises to keep in touch but we never heard from him again. We concluded that you obviously weren't interested in our business. We've gone elsewhere in the meantime and are very happy with the service we're getting".

Arrow(s) 4

These arrows represent the execution of the selling activity that turns an identified opportunity within a Qualified Prospect into a piece of work.

Brickwall 5

The activity here is represented by the image of the brick wall. The aim is to build relationships with key and valued clients to the point that it is unlikely that they will defect to our competitors. This is a huge subject that we will not attempt to cover in this publication. We have though, dedicated a whole book *Managing Key Clients*, to this subject.

Arrow(s) 6

If a client has drifted into being a 'problem child', the question is what are we going to do about it?

How to *plan* and *manage* the selling and marketing effort so that the right amount of the most effective activity (P1 to P5) needed to generate the 'right' number of high quality new clients for an individual and a firm actually happens - and happens in a consistent and continuous manner - is the subject of our third book *Growing Your Client Base*.

However, imagine the consequences of a large number of a firm's fee earners enthusiastically meeting and trying to 'sell' to many of the firm's best target clients - and doing it badly! Perhaps they come across as pushy, arrogant, uninterested or just lacking confidence. They would not only be unsuccessful at winning business today, they would also potentially be damaging the firm's reputation and destroying business for the future. The *skills and approaches* involved in making the most of those vital and precious first meetings with potential clients, and then in confidently and skillfully winning profitable work from those organisations (however long that process takes) are the subject of the remaining chapters in this book.

Section 2 **Selling - Building the Motivation to Buy**

Chapter 2 **Building the Motivation to Buy**

What is Selling?

To many professionals 'selling' is a dirty word. They base their views on the experience of being sold to badly by pushy salespeople who appear to be interested only in making a sale. Very few professionals would like to be seen as pushy by their clients or anyone else.

How then do we reconcile client-focused, and totally professional, business development and client engagement with selling?

Let's start by defining our terms. There are numerous definitions of selling. The dictionary tells us:

To sell: To persuade others to accept

That seems simple and reasonable enough.

However at PACE we are uncomfortable with one of the words included in this definition. That word is "persuade". If I feel my job is to persuade you then I will be tempted to do so by the force of my argument and by my genuine 'enthusiasm' for what my firm does. Unfortunately if you are not immediately persuaded I might be tempted to 'persuade' you harder. Then persuasion can become pushiness or pressure and pressure in this situation is usually counterproductive and leads to resistance.

Also if my job is to persuade you then all of the energy in the interaction will tend to come from me. If I am to be successful I need the energy to come from you. I want the energy to come from you. I need you to really **want** to move forward in the relationship - to **want** to engage with me; to **want** to consider my ideas positively; eventually to **want** to buy and to continue to buy from me. I don't want you to be persuaded - I want you to be motivated.

Our definition of selling is therefore:

To sell: To build the motivation to buy

If my job is building someone's motivation over time - not too quickly but also not too slowly - rather than trying to persuade them to do something, I can learn a lot from my experiences in motivating others in my management role - and my experiences, good and bad, of my manager trying to 'motivate' me!

The best people managers do and say the things that get people in their teams to want to do the things that will make them, and the team, successful. The good ones are able to do this because they understand some key facts about motivation. These include:

1. Everyone is unique. No two people are motivated by identical things.

2. To motivate someone you need to understand what 'makes them tick'. Not just what they do but *why* they do it. Not just what they *say* but what they *mean*.

3. If you try to motivate others by what motivates you, you will almost certainly not succeed. Many people will not be motivated by your actions - some will even be demotivated.

4. It is useless to make value judgements about what people should be motivated by. The manager needs to understand each person's mind and motivations in detail and then to work with what is, not what he or she would like to be.

5. In order for the manager to get to the point where his or her team is comfortable to be open about their motivations and feelings he or she must build a relationship with them, really listen to them and build confidence and trust.

In building the motivation to buy and re-buy (i.e. motivation in selling and creating new clients rather than in management) the lessons from the above list include:

1. Beware using the same argument (or features, benefits, proposal pages or slides) for two clients or potential clients. If you find yourself saying the same things to different people - or cutting and pasting chunks of proposals into others - you are acting as though you believe those people are the same. They are not.

2. The key to success lies in understanding what makes each (person in each) client tick - not just understanding what they **need**.

3. If you spend your time telling people what **you** believe is great about your expertise or service you will put off many clients. You will in fact come across as the very pushy salesperson we all so despise.

4. Don't moan about clients making 'stupid decisions' based on lack of understanding. Work with what the client sees and believes - and build the kind of relationship that allows you to influence her thinking before you need to put forward your solution.

5. Focus efforts on building trust and understanding. Invest most of your time in this and, in general, seek first to understand before seeking to be understood.

Much of success is therefore based on understanding the client and what makes her buy.

Why do People Buy?

What is it that makes a client choose one supplier and not others?

How is it that some people make a 'poor choice' when seemingly better competing offers are ignored?

As our careers in selling and business development have progressed, we have been exposed to various models and theories. Interestingly the vast majority of these models focus heavily on building selling behaviours rather than working hard to understand buying behaviours.

Over the years we have been told that:

- People buy if they buy you

- People buy if you can fulfil their needs

- People buy if you can lead them to the conclusion that they have needs which must be addressed and that they really are looking for a solution to these newly discovered (and now apparently mountainous) needs

- People buy for two reasons - because they need something or because it makes them feel good

- People buy if you can satisfy their needs and their wants

We have found that none of these are incorrect - but they all fall short in some regard. This sometimes comes into focus on a training session when a participant claims that, "I worked hard to understand every aspect of his needs, I checked it with him, I built the solution totally in line with what he said, and then he went and bought a solution with half the functionality and paid more for it. Tell me why that is."

The consultant who is working to the model of 'needs based selling' is struggling here. His initial thoughts are to doubt the participant's skill in understanding and fulfilling the client's needs. However, as the consultant works with more and more people he hears the story more and more often. These people can't all have done such a bad job. Perhaps the model of 'needs based selling' is incomplete?

Needs and Wants

A few years ago when the children of one of the authors were young and his job required him to carry a lot of bulky equipment around the country he looked at a 'people carrier' vehicle as a potential purchase. They were comfortable, gave good visibility, were reasonably economical, could carry a lot of equipment, were useful for transporting the family and dogs and were configurable so that weekend DIY jobs and shopping excursions could be accomplished quite easily. They were also well made, had received good reports in the motoring press and fell within his budget.

When it came time to change his car what did he buy? I think you can guess the answer. His sporty solution fulfilled very few of his logical needs and he had to personally top up the budget by a few thousand pounds. So much for needs based buying behaviour. What he needed and what he wanted were two different agendas.

Needs, Wants and Trust

Let us take as another example the purchase of a pension as provision for old age. Our case will be John, a 26 year old man, married for one year and who has just found out that he and his wife have a child on the way. They are delighted. John is not an irresponsible individual, he works but he does not have any pension provision in place.

One day John is introduced to a person who sells (amongst other financial services products) pensions. This person sits down with him and runs through various assumptions. When would he like to retire ideally? What would he like his lifestyle to be when he is retired? How long after retirement will he probably need to maintain this lifestyle?

The conclusion is reached that John will need to earn enough in the next 34 years to keep him in the style he is accustomed for the next 60 years! That is some conclusion. Even more startling is the calculation that he has just over 400 pay cheques (i.e. opportunities to contribute to pension provision) to come in the rest of his working life - assuming he is never out of work.

Does our 26 year old want to live frugally for the last third of his life? No way. Does he need a pension? You bet. Does he go ahead and take out a pension? No, he doesn't.

Why?

After the pensions salesman has gone John sits down with his wife. They have a budget of sorts and they have aspirations of the things they want to do in life - some long term, mostly shorter term.

They want to take a holiday the month after next - the last they'll have before they have children. They want to redecorate in expectation of the new arrival. They want to buy a very attractive and expensive pram which they have seen in a local store. They want to have another child within a reasonably short time of the first.

Do they need all these things - really need them? No - but they want them.

With all these priorities, the money which the pension would consume, just can't be considered right now. However, John has made a mental note that he will get some form of pension provision underway before he allows himself the luxury of a motorcycle.

When the salesman calls back to see John, John tells him that he and his wife have decided not to go ahead. The salesman re-iterates the calculations and arguments of their last meeting. John seems to waver but holds his ground. He decides to explain in detail the things he and his wife discussed and the priorities they have. It is clear however that the salesman is not interested in these issues in John's life. He keeps interrupting with the logical arguments. It is clear he is not listening to John. In the end John finishes the meeting with, "I understand what you're saying, but not now!"

The salesman leaves.

John is thinking, "I understood what he said, but not now - and as far as he is concerned - not ever!" John has decided that even if the pension was far enough up his priority list to go ahead, he would not buy from this person. This salesman displayed behaviours that indicated that he was more interested in selling something than understanding his potential client. Instinctively John does not trust this behaviour and people who seem to manifest this type of behaviour.

Some years on, John does conclude that the time is ripe to make pension provision for himself. He has been convinced of the need for years - now he wants to make this a priority. All he has to do is find the right person whom he feels he can trust to give him advice.

He wants to talk with someone who is very knowledgeable on the subject of pensions, someone who has a track record of advising people just like himself, someone who will listen to what he wants, someone who is not pushy, someone who will point him in the direction of the product most aligned to his situation - not their commission cheque - and preferably someone whom he can get on with. After all, there may be times in the future when his situation may change and he doesn't want to have to go through the process of finding a new adviser every time that happens.

Conclusion

Why do people buy? People buy because the product or service they decide to purchase fulfils a combination of their needs and wants and they feel they can trust the person and organisation who is supplying them.

Does this apply to every purchasing decision in life? No it does not. The more the transactional nature of the purchase, the less the concept will apply in totality.

In the vast majority of instances when prospective clients are considering the use of professional advisers, they are aware that this is not a transaction. This will be a relationship - for the duration of the project or perhaps a lot longer. When we position our offering we must be able fulfil the client's needs and meet their wants but do this in a way or through a process which enables the prospective client to trust us - to know that we are credible, capable and compatible with them.

The model as to why people buy is becoming more complete.

How new is all this?

It's not. In fact it is nearly 2500 years old.

In the early democracy of Greece, in both the Ecclesia (or Assembly) and the Council of Five Hundred, men had to justify their actions to their fellow citizens. The Assembly was also a place of deliberative rhetoric - where men urged the city to take one course of action or another. The law courts of the time could have a 'jury' of up to five hundred citizens. The state did not have the monopoly on prosecutions. All who could establish a prima-facie case could bring their opponents to trial.

In this environment it is hardly surprising that the ability to influence through oratory was considered to be highly important. The skill was so prized it was considered to be the second most important a man could possess. Only the skills of the warrior were considered to be more valuable.

The skills needed to influence others were studied in detail and around 330 BCE Aristotle captured the essence of persuasive behaviour in writing The Art of Rhetoric. This writing defines the high point in Greek oratory.

Aristotle defined what it was that made people believable and persuasive; what it was that enabled some to sell their ideas better than others. He identified three key characteristics in persuasive rhetoric. In Greek these are Logos, Pathos and Ethos.

What Aristotle was saying is that to be successful in influencing others we must produce arguments which, when people hear them, are rational and logical. This is Logos.

However, this is not enough. People also respond to emotional appeals - just as people buy based not just on logic but also on emotion - what they would like to have, not just what they need to have. This is Pathos.

If the person who appeals to people's logical needs and emotional wants is also someone who is considered to have a believable and trustworthy character (this is Ethos) then this person will be successful in their attempts at persuasion.

"Of those proofs... there are three kinds. Some reside in the character of the speaker, some in a certain disposition of the audience and some in the speech itself, through its demonstrating or seeming to demonstrate.

Proofs from character are produced whenever the speech is given in such a way as to render the speaker worthy of credence - we more readily and sooner believe reasonable men on all matters in general and absolutely on questions where precision is impossible and two views can be maintained.

... Proofs from the disposition of the audience are produced whenever they are induced by the speech into an emotional state.

... Finally, proof is achieved by the speech, when we demonstrate either a real or an apparent persuasive aspect of each particular matter."

Aristotle
The Art of Rhetoric

However, all people are different and on different occasions people will be motivated by different things. Therefore to be successful in selling, the most effective mix of emotional appeals and logical arguments has to be defined. The only person who has this information is the client. The person who wishes to sell his services therefore has to define from the client exactly what they would like.

We are always being told how difficult it is to prize a client away from an incumbent adviser. This is true. Even when the client goes out to tender, the incumbent is rightly considered to be in pole position to win the work next time. (This assumes that the reason for going out to tender is not dissatisfaction with the incumbent adviser.)

When we examine this behaviour in the light of the Aristotelian model it is easy to explain why. If the incumbent has been doing a half decent job for the client they will have the advantage of:

• Being a known, and therefore trustworthy, provider

    We often meet professionals who when told that a client has decided to stick with their existing advisers, have heard the words, "Better the devil you know than the devil you don't"

• Knowing the less tangible appeals which will persuade individuals in the client's organisation to support their proposal

    By spending time with the client's people, the incumbent professional has the opportunity to be perceived as someone who is credible, competent and compatible. If he achieves this, he becomes trusted. This trust gives the professional the opportunity to get to know the people behind the decisions.

He gets to know their likes and dislikes, their hopes and aspirations, their desires and their fears.

These factors do not appear in the Invitation to Tender.

Person A in the decision making process may want a solution which not only meets all of the organisation's rational needs but is also going to be positioned in such a way that the success of the solution's implementation will reflect upon him.

Person B may be looking at potential solutions and considering how much personal time and involvement she is going to have to commit. The more time and involvement, the worse the solution to the individual concerned.

Person C may be looking at potential providers from the point of view of personal security. If the last two projects in which this person has been involved have gone off the rails in a career threatening way, then this will motivate him to support the safest looking option.

All of the competing firms given the 'even playing field' of the Invitation to Tender do not have the advantage of this vital decision influencing information. The incumbent who has used his time well - and any prospective provider who has been 'courting' this client with interest and passion over a period of time - has the benefit of being in a position to craft a solution which not only meets the stated needs expressed in the Invitation to Tender, but also meets the more subtle and hidden wants of important people involved in the decision making process.

Richard Carlson in his book *Personal Selling Strategies for Consultants and Professionals* expressed this concept in the following way:

> "You will never make a serious error in judgement if you expect your prospects and clients to make decisions on personal rather than organisational consequences".

The following (very honest!) feedback from two clients who were recently involved in selecting a professional provider would suggest that Carlson may not be overstating the case:

* "It was like being on a jury. All the evidence was laid out before us and then the decision was made on pure emotion or gut instinct"

* "We really made the decision quickly and unanimously. And it was on gut feeling - although most of us would not admit it!"

Clients will always explain their appointment decisions in logical and rational terms but many of the key deciding factors may well be personal and emotional.

Real Needs and Perceived Needs

There are times when a client articulates her need quite clearly but when we explore further into the issue we begin to realise that this need is badly specified. It may simply be wrong! This often comes about when the client sees the symptoms of a problem but fails to recognise the root causes. The professional however, having dealt with these types of issues many times in the past, comes to the conclusion that there is a disparity between:

• What the person perceives as their need

• The real need

For example:

Client: I'm looking for help for my business developers. We're not
                            converting enough of our proposals sent to new prospects into work.
                            We need help to improve our proposal writing.

The need is explicit. The prospective client has said that she needs help of some sort
in producing better proposals. A few questions later the professional is convinced that
whatever the quality of the proposals being produced, this is not the underlying problem.
It is more fundamental. It has to do with the whole way the client organisation is
approaching new business development. This flawed process is being driven and endorsed
by the person sitting in front of him - the same person who has wrongly identified the
issue her business faces.

What does the professional do? Go along with the client's definition of the problem
and produce a solution which the client is likely to buy? Tell, or lead the client to the
conclusion that she is wrong and risk the person being offended or losing face - and
thereby ruin the professional's chance of ever winning work from this organisation?

The right answer is to only address real needs, and deal with real issues. However, we
have come across professionals who openly admit to taking on work initially addressing
the client's perceived needs then, as the project develops, changing the perception of the
requirement in the client's mind.

This can work. There is a very real explicable reason why it does work. However, there
are clear dangers in this approach and any professional adopting this way ahead must also
be prepared for the consequences of dealing later with a disgruntled client who believes
that the work was taken under false pretences.

If a professional is going to lead the client to the conclusion that her diagnosis is wrong,
how will this person have to be positioned to be believed? Quite simply, the client is
going to have to trust the professional's judgement more than her own.

Trust (Ethos) is not gained easily or quickly - it has to be earned, and mostly this takes
some time. Again, the incumbent adviser with a successful track record is in a better
position to challenge the client's assumptions. The new, unproven professional has to find
ways of building trust before seriously challenging the assumptions and without seeming
to confront the client.

The dangerous tactic of taking work initially aimed at addressing perceived needs,
then later changing the client's perception, can be successful because the client has
the opportunity to get to know the professional. If this 'getting to know you' period
is successful, then the adviser's **credibility, competence and compatibility** - the
cornerstones of trust - are established. The professional is then in a position to persuade
from this platform of trust.

However the best course of action is for the adviser to develop trust through the process of selling. In this way the client will achieve the best solution and the professional avoids the risk of destroying trust by 'changing his story half way through the project'.

In Summary

If we can present logical arguments to most effectively answer the real needs whilst also presenting solutions that satisfy the wants - and we are perceived to be a trusted character - we are likely to have a high level of success.

To understand the client's wants and be in a position to influence the client's perception of their real needs we must have earned a position of trust. Trust is fundamental to success in selling professional services.

In brief:

Perceived Needs

The needs that the client thinks she has. These needs will have been reached through 'logical' thought. However, the logic may be flawed or the information base on which the logic is founded may have shortcomings.

Real Needs

Real Needs may be an exact replica of the perceived needs or they may be very different. A client may specify logically what she wants but when these ideas are put to the 'expert' adviser, the solution sought by the client may not serve her well.

Wants

The desires which the client would like to have fulfilled by the purchasing decision.

The wants may be parallel to the perceived needs (e.g. "I want to be seen to be making a financially prudent decision or my credibility is on the line.")

The wants may be contradictory to the needs. (E.g. "I know we need to appoint a good adviser but I also want one based in Paris to give me the excuse to visit there more often.")

Trust

The state which the professional adviser reaches when he has proven to the satisfaction of the people within the client organisation that he is credible, competent and compatible with them.

The Iceberg Principle

The Iceberg Principle shows these concepts in a pictorial way. The tip of the iceberg, the small part which appears above the waterline represents people's behaviour. What lies under the waterline are the reasons for that behaviour. It is easy to observe behaviour and accept it at face value. However, if we work in any role which involves a lot of human interaction we will be more successful if we also know what drives the behaviour.

When we first talk with people we do not know well, people tend to express to us the things which appear factual. They focus on the tangible. They tend to speak of things which are easy to articulate and do not require deep explanation or justification. We may find in the fullness of time that appearances are deceptive. The factual may be fictitious, the logical may just be rationalisation with the benefit of hindsight.

Figure 2.1 The Iceberg Principle

People express the: Factual
                           Tangible
                           Easy to articulate
                           Easy to justify

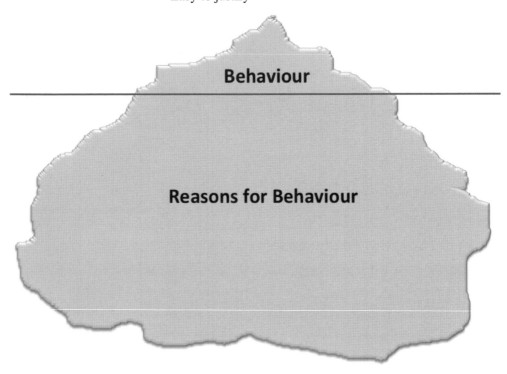

We need to understand the: Hidden motivators
                             Intangible
                             Difficult to articulate
                             Emotional drivers

When we get to know people we understand their 'hidden' motivators, they talk of things which are more intangible and difficult to articulate. We begin to glimpse the emotional (and sometimes irrational) drivers.

Henry Ford is credited with saying, "People have two reasons for doing anything - the right reason and the real reason."

In our Aristotelian model the tip of the iceberg represents the Perceived Needs - those the professional gets to learn very easily. Underneath the iceberg however are the more personal Wants. These usually take time to learn. The Real Needs we depict as a floating mass. The real needs may be a replica of the Perceived Needs. On the other hand they could be far removed from them.

Figure 2.2

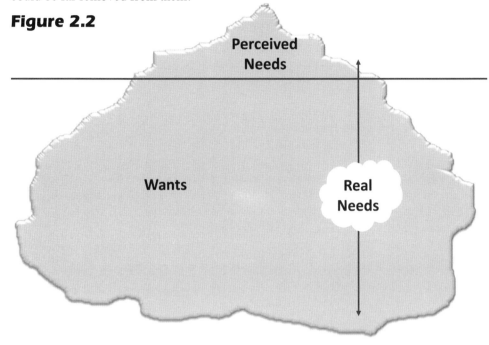

The key factor which allows us to get closer to understanding the Wants and to dealing with the Real Needs is the depth of Trust built up between the professional and the client. The deeper the trust the better the opportunity for understanding.

Figure 2.3

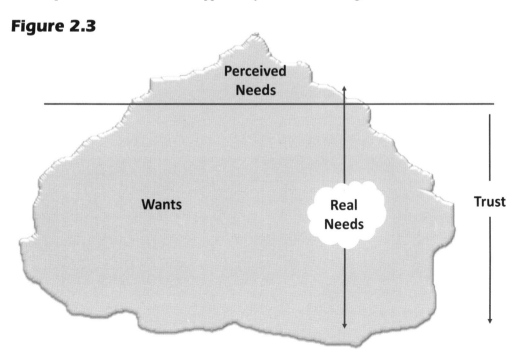

Building trust

"What you are shouts so loudly in my ears I cannot hear what you say"
Ralph Waldo Emerson

To earn a position of trust in the prospective client's eyes we need to build an image of credibility, competence and compatibility. To do this well and in a consistent and repeatable fashion we need to understand the types of behaviour that contribute to this positive impression. A number of these behaviours are detailed below.

Credibility

Factors influencing perceived credibility are:

Confidence

People who seem in control and confident in what they say and do are more believable than people who appear to be hesitant and uncertain. There is no one instant solution to having confidence. Real confidence comes from sustained success and sustained success comes as a result of applying many of the factors that appear below.

It also comes from being in a situation which we recognise and where we have experience of providing valuable solutions in the past. This in turn is likely to be more pronounced if we are focusing in a defined market whose issues we know well and where we have already had success.

Initial 'Impact'

People are never more sensitive (even if much of it is at a sub-conscious level) than when they first meet. We 'read' the other person's behaviour and we may have indelible impressions of them even before they have taken a seat in the meeting. The behaviours involved in initial impact are observable and can be controlled and improved.

Honesty

A lack of total honesty may take some time to be discovered or it could be discovered the moment a few words have been uttered. In either case nothing destroys credibility more quickly than dishonest behaviour.

Delivering as Promised

This is a factor influencing credibility that is not easily demonstrable early in the relationship. However, as a relationship with a client develops there are multiple opportunities to deliver (or fail to deliver). Continued credibility rests on being able to deliver on an ongoing basis.

Competence

Factors that affect perceived competence are:

Knowledge

Knowledge is defined in this context as the amount that we know (technically or theoretically) about a subject. Our qualifications (if recognised by a client) may give an indication of knowledge.

Track Record

If the client believes that we have a record of providing valuable advice in her particular industry and type of business, this will build our competence in her eyes. Most clients do not want to act as an educator of their professional advisers - and pay for the privilege of doing so. Clients are very astute in the main in assessing if advisers have a real track record personally or whether the track record is owned by their firm.

Expertise

Expertise is the ability to apply one's knowledge and track record to the client's particular situation and produce credible and believable ideas, ways forward and solutions. The client is picking up the message, "I have this knowledge, I've done this before, let me tell you the best way forward for you from here."

Insightful (Non Manipulative) Questioning

Questions that really get the client to think in a dimension which she had never considered before, can be a real demonstration of credibility. However, this type of questioning has to be applied with great skill as there is a danger that the professional can be seen to be leading the prospective client in a pre-determined direction in which the professional has a vested interest.

Compatibility

Factors influencing perceived compatibility are:

Genuine Interest

This is demonstrated through spending time with the client and getting to know and understand her business, the key players in the business and the issues and opportunities faced by the business. Questioning is vital in this process but there is no substitute for time invested.

(Active) Listening

To demonstrate that we have developed a real understanding of a client and the person's business, we must demonstrate that we have listened to, and absorbed, the messages that the other person has been transmitting to us.

Adapting Behaviour

"Just be yourself" is the worst piece of advice to give anyone who has the job of developing business from a wide range of people. The way we interact with a person running a wholesale vegetable business may well be different to the way we speak and behave with someone who runs a law firm. People who have difficulty in adapting their behaviour from their normal model find it more difficult to build a feeling of compatibility with a wide range of client types.

Showing Vulnerability

People rarely warm to the 'know-all'. Professionals need to be aware of this. Professionals spend their lives being right. That is what they get paid for. However, projecting an aura of never being wrong, an aura of impersonal computer-like unchallengeable accuracy, is going too far.

Occasionally saying, "That's my mistake," or "I'm sorry," can have a positive effect on developing a relationship. If the client comes to the conclusion that, "He never admits he's wrong, even when he clearly is," the professional is displaying behaviour unlikely to build any compatibility.

Figure 2.4

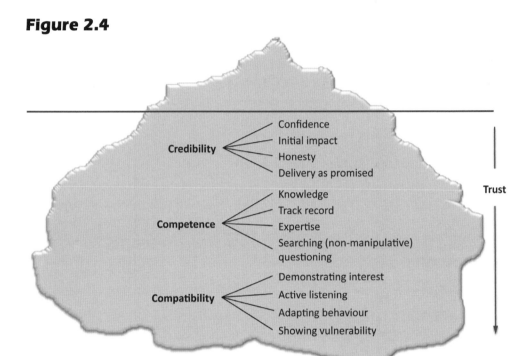

There is one further element in building trust - Consistency.

Consistency

We have already suggested that the behaviours involved in building and maintaining Credibility, Competence and Compatibility need to be demonstrated not just once but consistently. There are three dimensions of consistency:

- Consistency over time;
- Consistency towards people; and
- Consistency between people

Consistency over time

When we are building a new relationship time will tell whether the behaviours described above are deeply held and well practised or whether they are skin deep and applied purely for our own (short term) gain.

Consistency in how we engage with new clients and contacts - whether or not there is an immediate opportunity for work - will be noticed by the person themselves and by others who observe our behaviour. Trust is about belief. Consistency, or lack of it, will build or undermine that belief.

Consistency towards people

In business development meetings one of our ex-colleagues always focused his attention on the 'most important' person (client) in the room to the exclusion of others. As you might imagine those 'less important' individuals felt disengaged from him and from the ideas, solutions and proposals he eventually put forward. This worked against him when those other influencers had a real say in the decision and/or when the main decision maker noticed and was put off by his behaviour - i.e. in just about every situation!

This was a behaviour we tried hard to change in this colleague.

Consistency between people

Nobody expects consultants in an organisation to be clones of each other! However if their behaviour is inconsistent and the style, messages and approach are very different, clients and potential clients may be confused and find it difficult to know "what to believe". If everyone at the firm is consistent in the important elements of client development - while still being true to themselves - it will be easier for the client to build and maintain high levels of trust and belief in the organisation and all its representatives.

Some of the ways of building trust can be learned. They are skills or knowledge based. However some of the factors which build trust, particularly those which fall under the compatibility heading, cannot be achieved through pure technique. Technique is not enough. It is the core values of the professional and how these values map with the prospective client which can have a major impact.

Can anyone learn the techniques of selling? The answer is 'Yes'. However, the most successful people will not only have a sound application of the techniques required, they will also have the character and core values which appeal to the majority of people with whom they come into contact.

No, thank goodness, sincerity cannot be faked.

Building the motivation to buy - the 'selling meeting'

As we explained in Chapter 1 when we looked at each of the activities that are needed to build a pipeline of future work, an initial meeting with a target client has three potential outcomes. One outcome is that we decide that the prospect is not worth further pursuit. The second is that further pursuit is desirable but there are no immediate opportunities in sight therefore we will have to maintain contact through on-going marketing and relationship building activities. The third is that we see an opportunity for work in either the short or medium term and we believe that it is appropriate to begin pursuit of this opportunity.

It is the evidence that we gather at the very first meeting that we have with a Defined Prospect that allows us to make the right decision as to the best way forward. This meeting is therefore critical. It is critical for another reason as well. In our first paragraph we have been very self-centric - *we* will make the decision as to the way that *we* will proceed. There is a danger that we may forget one other important party - the prospective client. She may have something to say about the way forward. Just as we are forming a picture that will allow us to make a decision as to the best way ahead for us, so also is the client. Just like us the prospect is gathering evidence from the very outset - from the very first handshake in the reception area.

As the meeting progresses the prospective client can come to a number of conclusions. For example she may conclude:

- These people seem OK so far so I will tell them about immediate work that they may be able to do. They could be another string to the bow but I won't do anything to enhance their chances over anyone else that I'm talking with

- These people have really impressed me so far so I will tell them about immediate work that they may be able to do. I'll give them a really good brief and be very open as I have an early feeling that they may be good to work with at some point

- These people have impressed me but we have nothing on the horizon in the areas that they appear to work in however I would have no objection to keeping in touch

- These people are unimpressive and don't measure up to the kind of advisers that we are using today. Even if we have work that their firm could do I don't want to become involved in a discussion with them about it

Quite clearly we want to make the kind of impression that leads a client to thinking the second option and never considering the fourth.

What can go wrong?

Our marketing has done its job. The Defined Prospect has agreed to a first meeting. A chance now to sell our services! Let's think what may be appropriate. What would they be most interested in? We should start by telling them about .... Stop!!

This is where so many professionals go wrong. They see this meeting as a selling opportunity (right) and therefore their job is to pitch to the prospect in order to convince her that their firm has the services and capabilities that she should use in the future - wrong!

Let's look at it from the Defined Prospect's point of view. She has been on the receiving end of our marketing activities and approaches over a period of time. One or two things made an early impression so she continued to notice our stuff. She thought that a lot of it was good and mostly it was relevant to her. She then received an intensive campaign and could deduce easily that we were a firm that wanted to make a big impression and that clearly wanted to take the discussion further. When we called her up she said that, based on what she had seen to date, she was open to an exploratory meeting but that we had to realise that she used other advisers for the kinds of work that she understood that we did. We said, "Fine, we would expect that, but let's meet anyway". She said, "OK".

Let's also think what will be in the client's mind the day she decides (hopefully) to appoint our firm to carry out the first piece of work for her. She will have reached the point where she is thinking, "I trust these people with this case and I think my organisation and I can work with them". Now, the simple fact is that most people do not reach this conclusion at the end of a one hour meeting, no matter how well we have managed it.

So, based on everything we have looked at in this chapter, how do we get a prospective client to the point where she says, "I trust you and want to work with you and your firm"?

1. Firstly we must accept that (except in unusual circumstances) this feeling will never be created within a prospective client in just one meeting. The number of contacts required is indeterminate. It will depend on the nature of the client and the nature of the type of work that we are trying to win. The more 'mission critical' the work or the more it impacts personally on the people giving the instructions the longer the process is likely to take, as there is greater level of trust that needs to be developed.

2. Secondly we create trust by demonstrating to the client over a period of time that we have competence and credibility and that we are compatible with her and her business.

This could take a lot of effort - but let us return to our original premise. Our Defined Prospects are other firms' clients. Moreover, if our selection criteria are working well they will be the *key* clients of these other firms. The very best of these competitors may have key client plans in place aimed at building the strength of their relationships month on month, year on year. We are going to have to be very good to win work from these entrenched incumbents and to be very good we are going to have to put in a lot of effort. And, we have to get the first meeting right!

Structuring the First Meeting

Let us assume that we have agreed with the target client that for our first meeting we need an hour. Our experience tells us that most prospective clients are unwilling to give more than an hour to an initial exploratory meeting. The exception to this is where the adviser comes with a high recommendation from someone for whom the prospect has high regard.

How should this hour ideally be used? The hour should follow the PACES process and should be split roughly as shown to the right. Assume that the meeting starts on the hour.

Figure 2.5

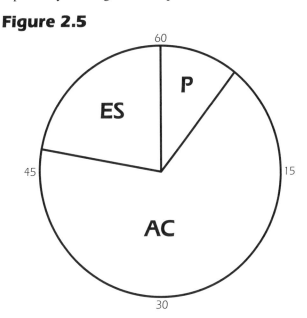

The elements of the PACES process are as follows.

P   Position ourselves and our organisation

A   Ascertain in detail the prospective client's situation and requirements

C   Confirm to the prospect our understanding of their situation and requirements

E   Explain or explore a suitable way forward - based on what has gone before in
            the meeting

S   Seek commitment to the suggested way forward

'P'

The 'P' part of the meeting is the first five minutes referred to earlier. In reality this can
extend to seven or eight minutes but should never be allowed to go on any longer than
ten. In these few minutes we are introducing the firm and ourselves, engaging in the
appropriate amount of 'chit-chat', setting the scene and agreeing the purpose and direction
of the meeting with the prospective client.

'AC'

The 'AC' part of the meeting should take up the bulk of the time available. It is in this part
of the meeting that we are building an understanding of the Defined Prospect's business
today, where it is going in the future and the kind of requirements that she may have of
professional firms like our own. We are trying to create a picture in our own mind of the
prospect's needs and wants. We are also developing a feeling as to whether this client
and the type of work that she is looking for in the future from firms like ours fits with our
aspirations and strengths.

If it looks like this is a relationship that we want to take forward we are also trying to gain
information that will enable us to progress our business development activities in the most
effective way.

In this phase of the meeting we are listening to the prospective client and prompting her
with questions some of which we have prepared prior to the meeting. Not only are we
listening but we are actively listening - meaning that we are not coming to conclusions
about what we have been told until we have checked our understanding with the prospect.
Yes, all this in about 40 minutes!!

'ES'

On the assumption that what we have learned to this point has whetted our appetite to take
the relationship further, in the last ten to 15 minutes of the meeting we should:

*   Give the prospective client two or three really cogent arguments as to why our firm
    may be of value to her in the future - based not on generic arguments but related back
    directly to what we have been told over the past 40 minutes or so

- Suggest a way ahead - or put a couple of alternatives forward for the client to choose from. These suggestions should meet three criteria. Firstly they should not be difficult for the prospective client to agree to. Secondly they should involve the prospect in some form of action - even if it is simply to meet again. Thirdly they should in some way keep us in direct face to face contact with the client and her organisation

- Gain agreement to the suggested way forward

In the next three chapters we look in detail at the skills necessary for success in each element of the PACES process.

Section 3 **PACES - The Steps to Successful Selling**

Chapter 3 **P**ACES: Position Ourselves and Our Organisation

Before The Meeting Begins

Not surprisingly, many professionals feel uncomfortable and ill-at-ease before an initial meeting with a prospective client. For many this is not common ground. Most client contact is with people we know, in many cases with people we know well. Not only are we meeting someone for the first time, we are asking the professional to carry out a job which is not day-to-day practice. This is the most difficult scenario of all - conducting a 'selling' meeting with a prospect.

The chances of 'failure' appear high. Some professionals, thinking back to previous experiences, *know* that the prospect of 'failure' is high. Unfortunately some professionals unwittingly decrease their own chances of success by engaging in behaviours that diminish their standing in the eyes of the prospective client. The development of an image of competence, credibility and compatibility begins before the visit is made and is clearly transmitted in the first couple of minutes of the face-to-face contact. The knowing professional behaves in the following way.

1. Prepare, prepare, prepare

In our workshops we continue to be surprised by professionals who openly admit to finding difficulty with initial meetings with prospective clients and tell us in the next breath about preparing in the car outside the premises or 'remaining flexible and playing it by ear'.

If we have defined the prospect as an organisation that has the makings of a potential profitable client, then we owe it to ourselves to prepare as well as we possibly can. There is more publicly available information on companies than ever before. If we wish to display competence in front of the prospect then we ought to know something about their business. Also, if we already know much of what is in the public domain about the organisation before we arrive, we can spend as much as possible of the meeting on what we cannot research, i.e. the mind (views, perspectives, priorities) of the person we are meeting. The fact that we have made the attempt to find out also demonstrates a level of genuine interest.

A few of the places we should be looking for information and insight before the meeting include Google (obviously), company websites (particularly the 'Recruitment' page as it very often gives insights into how the organisation likes to see itself, its culture and what it sees as most distinctive about itself), Linked-In and other social media, sector media and contacts of ours in the marketplace. This may sound like a lot to do but, in our experience, one to two hours of focused research is usually enough.

We should use all this information to prepare:

- How we plan to open the meeting
- What areas we aim to explore in the meeting
- How we phrase some of the key questions we plan to ask in the meeting

Beware! We should refrain at this stage from trying to determine what we should try to sell to the prospective client. We have heard professionals preparing for meetings with new clients by discussing with colleagues "What do we think they might be interested in?" and "What should we talk to them about?". Such an early focus on possible solutions, based on limited information, very little insight and a whole host of unnoticed assumptions, can lead to myopia in the meeting and potential opportunities can be missed as the professional ploughs down a pre-determined but ultimately barren furrow. It will also get in the way of good listening.

The information we gain in our research is there to guide our exploration, not to decide what we should be selling.

2. Be on time

Such a guideline is so obvious - why mention it? We accept that it is a huge generalisation, but more than 60 years collective experience working in all manner of market areas convinces us that professionals are amongst the worst time managers in industry! Strange for a profession which has only time to sell.

The outcome is that lateness becomes habitual. Internal meetings never start on time, they never finish on time, people are perpetually behind the clock. The real problems start when this behaviour is visited on the client. One client of ours is a large insurance company. A new MD joined the organisation and early in his tenure he and his fellow directors were kept waiting on one occasion by one of the partners from the auditors. When he 'sounded off' about this behaviour, one of his fellow directors remarked that their auditors' people were always late and that they were forever sitting around waiting for them to show up to meetings. At this point the MD charged his people with counting every minute of management time which was wasted by the auditors. When the auditors sent their next invoice to the company for time spent working on various tasks, the new MD sent his own back in response - based on management time lost through the auditor's tardiness.

A very embarrassed and chastened senior partner finally settled the potentially explosive situation by negotiating a large reduction of the audit fee for the following year. Lateness can cost!

Some take the view that 10 or 15 minutes here or there is OK. The attitude is that after all we have to deal with congested roads and sometimes unreliable public transport. Some of our clients and potential clients don't see it that way. A 10 o'clock meeting to many means a meeting that starts at 10 o'clock - not a professional who rushes into reception at 10 o'clock. If the very first impression (even before we have met) is one of a person who can't even organise himself to get to a meeting on time we should not be surprised to have our credibility questioned. At the very first opportunity to deliver as promised, we have failed.

3. Think through, and control, our 'reception routine'

How do we want to feel when we walk through the office door of the managing director of our biggest prospective client: Cool? Calm? Collected? Confident? Comfortable? In control? Not too many would disagree with these descriptions. When we are waiting in reception areas we observe the behaviour of other visitors. Many of these visitors represent companies who would like to sell their goods and services to the organisation concerned. Some of the behaviours they adopt in reception could lead to pre-meeting feelings which would be best described as flustered, uncomfortable, unconfident and out of control.

Combining a number of oft-repeated scenarios this is what we can see. The language we use in all of our examples may not be yours. However, look beyond the words and focus on the underlying messages.

How not to do it

It is one minute to ten. A well-dressed, but somewhat out of breath, gentleman carrying a briefcase walks through the reception door. He is a salesman. He looks around getting his bearings. It is clear he has not visited this building before. He walks up to the reception desk where there are two receptionists. Their job is to answer the phone and divert calls to the correct extension and also to greet and sign in visitors.

Salesman	Good morning. I'm Malcolm Manning from Hermann Norris - I've got a meeting with John Jackson at 10.

His voice conveys the fact that he has been rushing to make the meeting. He sounds breathless.

Receptionist	Sorry?
Salesman	Malcolm Manning from Hermann Norris.
Receptionist	Sorry but I didn't get your name.
Salesman	I...

At this stage the telephone rings and the receptionist goes through her well-practised and professional routine of taking the call and ensuring it is introduced to the right person in the building. Meanwhile the salesman stands in front of the reception unit like a schoolboy in front of the headmaster's desk. He is thinking how stupid these people are. Don't they listen?

This must be the tenth time this week he's been through this rigmarole!

He has an important initial meeting with the marketing director, John Jackson, where he hopes to persuade Jackson to use his company for some promotional work in the future. He will have to be at his best as a communicator and at this stage he is having difficulty with yet another stupid receptionist who hasn't yet grasped his name. He is beginning to feel a little uncool.

The receptionist finishes diverting the call.

Receptionist   You have an appointment with Mr Jackson?

Salesman   That's right - Malcolm Manning from Hermann Norris.

The salesman looks at the receptionist. He feels unsure that she's got it right even this time.

The receptionist dials an extension number.

Receptionist   Judy? I've got a Mr Norris here to see John.

At this stage the salesman leans over and corrects the receptionist hoping that the secretary on the other end of the line will hear and realise the receptionist's error. After some confusion the salesman's name is established correctly.

Receptionist   Mr Jackson's secretary says that his previous meeting is over-running. She expects he will be free in ten minutes. In the meantime please take a seat.

The salesman turns to the corner of the reception area where there are two leather seats and a sofa. Despite the fact that he has sat in his car for the last hour, driving to this meeting, the salesman feels obliged to obey the receptionist's 'instructions'. As he takes one of the capacious chairs he wonders where people buy this type of furniture. The common characteristics of reception furniture, he concludes, are that it is low to the ground, extremely soft to the point that it nearly envelopes you and consequently is almost impossible to get out of.

After a few minutes the receptionist leans over the reception unit and says:

Receptionist   Mr Jackson sends his apologies but he will be a few minutes more. Would you like a cup of coffee while you are waiting?

The salesman feels it would be rude to refuse this hospitality, and besides, he has not consumed any caffeine since he left the Starbucks 10 minutes earlier.

Salesman   Yes please, that's very kind.

Five minutes later the receptionist hands the cup of hot coffee to the salesman. He struggles to take it from her. He has to try to sit up further in order to reach the cup and saucer. Not making the task any easier is the handful of record cards which the salesman has been sorting through on his lap.

You can probably anticipate what is going to happen next.

The coffee is very hot and very good. The salesman sips it in a comfortable reverie. He then becomes aware of a presence. The presence is manifested by a pair of size 12 shoes pointing directly toward him from a distance of three feet. The salesman looks straight ahead at the suited knees of a man.

Customer	Malcolm Manning?
Salesman	Yes.

He would like to continue with words like, 'Good to meet you', but such expressions normally follow the opening handshake.

He looks up to his customer who appears to be at least nine feet tall. He feels very small in comparison. He knows he needs to get out of this chair - but how? The low table is way out of his reach. He can't put his coffee cup down. Any sudden movement and he will be wearing hot coffee. That would be a great start! He begins to move in an upward direction. His notes fall off his lap and try to bury themselves down the side of the leather chair. He grabs at them. The coffee slops but fortunately does not spill.

The customer sees all this. He sees the discomfort of his guest and is embarrassed for him initially. It then crosses his mind that he is scheduled to share the next hour with this gauche creature. He wonders if there is any way in which he can reasonably foreshorten the meeting? Perhaps he could say that something has cropped up and could they keep the discussion to twenty minutes?

He realises that the salesman is not going to make it by himself.

Customer	Here, let me take that.

He reaches down and takes the cup and saucer from the salesman who then slides forward in the chair and pushes himself to his feet. The sitting and getting up positions have caused the salesman's shirt tails to come out of his trousers. Does he tuck them in or does he pretend that nothing is wrong and hope that they're not showing?

Once on his feet he is confronted by a man who is a little more than average height but certainly not the nine-foot giant originally observed.

Salesman	Good to meet you Mr Jackson.

The salesman offers his hand and the two of them shake. The customer takes care. A vigorous pumping of his right hand could cause him to spill coffee over his left hand. The salesman, sensitive as ever, recognises the customer's plight. There is a tinge of red in the salesman's cheeks and ears.

The salesman turns and picks up his briefcase in one hand and a folder in the other. Both he and the customer look briefly at the coffee cup.

Customer	I'll take this for you.

The words are said out of politeness. The last thing that the customer wants is to carry this cup and saucer on the two-minute walk to his office through four sets of swinging doors. They start walking. The salesman feels flustered, uncomfortable, unconfident and out of control. The customer wants this meeting out of the way.

Controlling our 'Reception Routine'

Time spent waiting in reception should be used well and the preventable errors demonstrated by our salesman are easily avoided with a little thought. Tips when in the reception area are:

1. We should introduce ourselves by giving our *business card* to the receptionist. No one can vouch for the receptionist's hearing or memory but you can bet she can read and work out which is the company and which is our name. People with a lot of soft vowels in their name or people with unusual names who refuse to allow a receptionist to look at their business card make life very difficult for these people.

2. Don't march up and down. This can make the receptionists uncomfortable. Move around though. There can be *a lot to see and observe in a reception area*. Some companies use it as their initial showcase because customers as well as suppliers visit. Read the certificates on the wall. What does this indicate about this company? Look at the brochures. What new information can we glean from these? Scan the press cuttings book. This will quickly indicate what activities the organisation is proud of. Read the company newspaper if there is one. What does the tone of this tell us about recent events within the organisation?

   We have often been asked the question: 'What do you talk about during that minute or two when you're walking from reception to the meeting room. You may be walking with the prospective client or it may be her secretary. The weather and car parking are rather banal. What subjects can you reasonably touch upon?'

   Our answer is a simple one. Make a point of arriving five to ten minutes before the agreed meeting time (more than this could be seen by the other person as some sort of cheap power tactic) and find something in reception which could be the basis of a short chat.

3. When it is important to be seen to be comfortable and controlled don't fall into the traps our salesman, Malcolm Manning, made for himself. Most times we do not have to wait more than 15 minutes or so. It is not too onerous to stay on our feet for this length of time. If the company is in the habit of offering coffee to guests in reception then it probably is generous enough to offer the same in meetings.

Remember, we are applying these guidelines to the early meetings with prospective clients. It is different with existing clients. We probably know the receptionist by name, she knows how we like our coffee, when we get stuck in the reception furniture we laugh about it and the client cracks a joke while helping to pull us out of the chair. Being able to make that first eye contact from a level position is simply not relevant. The relationship is already established.

But a first meeting *is* different. We have to demonstrate and earn our *credibility, competence* and *compatibility*.

At the Meeting

Let us take the most common scenario. We have arrived five minutes before the agreed meeting time and have checked in at reception. A couple of minutes later the secretary of the person we are to meet arrives in reception and invites us to follow her to her boss's office.

A yard from the door to her manager's office she steps aside and with a gesture indicates for us to walk into the room. In front of us is the great unknown!

This is the time when all of those dark memories can flood back. We can have visions of the most difficult person we ever met - the person who gave us a hard time from the moment we walked through the door - the person who seemed to want to personally humiliate us. We remember finishing such meetings feeling like we were a mugging victim.

Some years ago research was being carried out in New York into muggings and the victims of muggings. It appeared that there were people who lived in high crime areas who theoretically should have been subject to mugging attempts but had some kind of immunity. On the other hand there were individuals who were continual victims of muggers. Traditional groupings did not seem to explain the phenomenon. It was not a matter of size, sex or colour. As a part of the research, convicted muggers were taken to areas where muggings were known to occur. They were asked to point out people whom they would mug. Mostly they identified the same people. When asked why these people were selected, the most common feedback was: 'It's the way they move. It's something about their behaviour.'

The same applies to business meetings, in this case initial meetings between professionals and prospective clients. Usually the prospective client has the upper hand by being on home ground. They can call the shots. However, our observations totally convince us that the likelihood of being mugged in such a meeting is almost completely in the hands of the professional. If he displays the wrong behaviour and shows 'weakness' he leaves himself open to being a 'victim'.

People are never more sensitive to one another than when they meet for the first time. Consciously and subconsciously we are weighing up the other person. We all know the adage:

> You never get a second chance to make a good first impression.

It's true. If we get off to a poor start we may never recover.

If we are completely blunt, the opening of these types of meetings by professionals is weak. People tell us they feel uncertain about taking the initiative because they are on someone else's territory. They tell us they find it hard to put into words the reason they have come to see the prospective client - i.e. to sell her something. Yet in the majority of cases the professional has asked to meet with the prospect. The prospect is expecting the professional to tell her what the meeting is all about. The meeting typically wobbles to a start with little agreement to what is to be achieved or discussed.

It does not have to be this way. With some thinking and practice the professional can open this type of meeting in such a way that the prospective client is struck by an image of a person who has done this many times before, a person who is comfortable, confident and in control. The client is not made to feel they have to apologise for their guest's behaviour.

David Maister has some very telling thoughts about this phase of the meeting. From his article 'How Clients Choose' he says:

> "By the fact that you are sitting here talking to me, you can assume that you have successfully marketed your firm: now the time has come to sell yourself...
>
> Your selling task is to earn my trust and confidence - with the emphasis on the word 'earn'...

My impressions and perceptions are created by small actions that are meaningful for their symbolism, for what they reveal. How you behave during the interview will be taken as a proxy for how you will deal with me after I retain you. Unlike the process of qualification which is predominantly rational, logical and based on facts, the selection stage is mostly intuitive, personal and based on impressions..."

One very simple but effective guideline for opening this type of meeting with someone we have not met before, is to remember that the other person probably has three questions in her mind as the meeting gets under way. These questions are:

*   Who are you?
*   What is this all about and/or what is going to happen?
*   How long will it take?

The professional must walk into the meeting with a very specific plan as to how he is going to answer these (usually unspoken but very real) questions.

How to open the meeting - an example

Let us take one example of how the meeting could be opened in a very positive manner - demonstrating competence and credibility.

Gestured in by the secretary, the professional walks into the office without pausing. He is carrying his briefcase and meeting notes folder in his left hand. He sees the prospective client across the other side of his office and he smiles. The client is standing, obviously expecting his entrance.

Without stopping, the professional walks confidently and unhurriedly toward the client. As he nears the client he extends his right hand.

Professional   Kate Parkinson? I'm Ray Stringer from Wright and Tyler.

They shake hands. Stringer's handshake is firm but not crushing. It is dry. His meeting notes folder has been carried in his left hand which is clammy from the contact. He has his notes folder in his hand as he knows it will be needed from an early stage in the meeting. He has no intention of trying to find a convenient moment to dig the folder out of his briefcase when the meeting is under way.

Client   Nice to meet you Ray. Please take a seat.

The professional sits in the seat offered by the prospective client. It is opposite her desk.

At this point we would expect some 'chit-chat' or social conversation. How much is appropriate depends on two things, the culture of the country or region in which this meeting takes place and the preference/personality of the client. Some clients are unhappy at wasting more than a minute of their precious time, others prefer to get to know the person they are meeting before getting down to business. As Ray has not met this person before he does not know her preference. He should be aware of clues in her manner and her surroundings but, as a rule of thumb, he might engage fully in this type of conversation for a limited time, perhaps a couple of minutes in the UK. Then he should let the client continue to chat - and listen with real interest - for as long as she wants to but without 'stoking the fire' by adding too many of his own thoughts. The social conversation is then likely to subside gently and in a way that is comfortable to the client.

Once this point is reached it is vital that he takes the initiative. A pause at this point can lead to one of two comments from the client, either:

1. "Well, thanks for coming to see me. What do you think you can do for us?", or

2. "Thanks for coming to see me – let me tell you about us and then I would be interested in hearing what you have to offer".

The first request is obviously not what Ray wants to hear as it will either tempt him into a premature presentation based upon a lot of guesswork or he will have to attempt to change the client's mind by suggesting that he would like to understand more before he starts to give any answers. Even if he manages to do the latter he is already on the back foot and may only have managed to secure a brief 'stay of execution'.

The second comment appears much better – in fact it could seem exactly what Ray would like to hear. However his experience tells him that if the client starts to give him information at this stage she is likely to continue for a maximum of 10-15 minutes and will then expect a full-blown presentation on his firm and how they can help. What he really needs to do at this stage is to earn the right to explore the client's situation for up to 40 minutes and then to be in a position to put forward enough information to motivate the client to take the best next steps in the relationship. For this to happen he needs to establish his own credibility and his and his organisation's bona fides, set the scene for the meeting, agree how it will be structured and give the client really good reasons – not just why he wants to know more – but why it would be in her interests for him to understand the situation before he starts to put forward his thoughts or ideas. To do all this he must first take the initiative and then manage the next few minutes in a confident, fluent (but not robotic) and credible way.

Professional   Thank you very much for agreeing to see me.

With this the professional takes his business card from his folder and hands it to the prospective client.

Client   Here, let me reciprocate with one of mine.

Kate Parkinson opens the top drawer of her desk, takes out a business card and hands it to Ray Stringer. Stringer takes a moment to read the card. He knows that most people think long and hard about what they put on their cards and this can say a lot about them. He looks at how the name is given on the card, he looks at the person's title, he looks for the availability of the person by glancing to see how many telephone numbers are listed.

Professional   I think I owe you an apology. I wrote to you as the Financial
                      Director. I see you are the Financial and Administration Director.

His behaviour indicates that he is observant, that he is willing to demonstrate interest and that he is open and prepared to apologise if he is wrong. It has happened in seconds. As Maister observed: 'My impressions and perceptions are created by small actions that are meaningful for their symbolism...'

Client   It's a very recent development. The director responsible for
                      administration retired recently and the decision was to put it all under

one roof. There was a lot of cross-over between the two departments in any case. It's not a problem. I only got my new cards on Monday.

Professional   Good, because I was sure I had checked. Before we get under way can I just check the time we have together? When we spoke on the phone we agreed an hour.

Client   Could we keep it to 50 minutes? I have a meeting with the Marketing Director in exactly an hour and I'd like a few minutes' preparation time.

Professional   Sure - so we need to wrap up by ten minutes to the hour? If we're in the middle of something which is particularly of interest to you would it be OK to finish the discussion at some other time?

Client   I'm sure we could.

The professional knows the time boundaries of the meeting. More importantly the prospective client knows that he knows and that he has noted it. She will not begin twitching and turning off 40 minutes into the meeting, wondering how she can terminate the discussion. Subtly the professional has also indicated that he is used to working to timescales and deadlines. He knows that letting the meeting take as long as it takes is understood by many people to be pure arrogance. It assumes that the prospective client has nothing better to do than to spend her time with the professional.

Professional   As I said in our telephone conversation I would very much like to take the opportunity in this meeting to get to know your organisation. However before we get under way, could I ask you how much you know about my organisation, Wright and Tyler?

This is not an idle question. Stringer has met with people who have had all manner of conceptions and misconceptions about his firm. He knows that it is important right from the start that there are no misconceptions and that the client has a broad perspective of what his firm is about. This is an early opportunity to position his firm and to position himself. Besides, he knows that people like to know who they are talking to. The introduction of himself and his firm is basic good manners above all else.

Client   Well I do know the name. I know that you are accountants and tax specialists but not one of the Big 4. You sent me a lot of information but to be perfectly honest I have not found time to read it all.

Professional   Would it be helpful then if I gave you a short two-minute overview?

He knows it is important to get the prospective client's agreement to this. He also knows from experience that a good 'positioning statement' should last for one and a half to two and a half minutes. Less than a minute and a half and he won't make the best of his opportunity. More than two and a half minutes will sound long and the prospective client may start to turn off. He has chosen his words carefully. The client knows that this picture will be painted within a couple of minutes.

Client   Please.

Professional	Well, you're absolutely right that we are very strong in all areas of audit and taxwork. However, our expertise extends well beyond these areas too. We also offer professional advice in corporate recovery and corporate finance where we work with our clients and financial institutions to raise business capital. In addition to this we offer specialist consultancy advice to help solve business problems in the areas of Business Strategy, Information Technology, Marketing, and Human Resources.
	We are engaged by our clients for two reasons. Firstly there may be a statutory requirement - for instance the audit. The other reason, though, is that our clients are looking to develop some form of business advantage and do not have the capabilities employed in-house. It makes sense to utilise what they need, when they need it, through us.
Client	It sounds rather like our current auditors.
Professional	I am sure that is true. Where we do differ from other players in the marketplace is in our client focus. We specialise in working with growing businesses - businesses like yours that every now and again face new challenges that are brought about by crossing new thresholds. I notice, for example, that you recently made your first acquisition and also that you opened your first office outside the UK last year. We really understand these issues because we work with them daily. Therefore we can offer our clients the most appropriate help and support whether that emanates from one of our 20 UK offices or one of our offices abroad.
	Statistically we lead in this arena. In the recent past we have been the Reporting Accountants for more AIM flotations than any other organisation.
	While we have a wealth of experience in working with many growing business one of the things that experience tells us is that every one of those businesses is unique and that any expertise that we provide needs to be tailored to their specific requirements and to the specific opportunities and challenges they face at any particular time.
	As for me, I am a senior manager within the local Guildford office. My particular area of expertise is corporate tax and I've worked in this field for 15 years. However, I represent the entire firm and whilst some of the challenges faced by your organisation may be outside of my own particular area, once I know what is of interest I can introduce you to the correct person - or people - from Wright and Tyler. Does that give you an understanding of Wright and Tyler and how I fit into it?
Client	Yes, that has been helpful.

Professional	Good. As I mentioned earlier, we recognise that every organisation is unique so, rather than, at this stage, going into more detail of what we do and how we do it, some of which I believe would be very relevant to you and some that would be less so, I would value the opportunity of finding out more about your organisation so that towards the end of the meeting, and perhaps beyond, we can focus on those things that would be of most interest to you.
	How does that sound?
Client	Yes, that's fine but I also have one or two questions related to a personal taxation situation. Could we find some time, perhaps toward the conclusion of the meeting to discuss that?
Professional	Shall we say we tie up anything related to the business ten minutes before we have to finish and spend the remaining time on your questions?

He realises again the value of checking the prospect's agenda. He knows it is too easy to become fixated on what he wants to achieve out of the meeting and not meet the prospect's expectations.

Client	Sure, that should be long enough. I think it is fairly straightforward.
Professional	In that case would it be OK to start off by my asking you a few questions? I did some research earlier so I believe I know much of what is in the public domain, however what I would really like to understand is how you see things, now and in the future. Would you mind telling me...

The P of the PACES process is completed. The professional is now ready to move into the A and C part of the process. What is the image in the prospective client's mind?

She is probably thinking:

> Here's a person who knows what he's doing. He knows where he is starting, he knows where he is finishing and he knows what goes in-between. He's planned, he's done his homework, he's structured and organised, he's observant and he listens. He is assertive but not at all aggressive. He's credible and capable and is starting to demonstrate he wants to be compatible. He has made a good initial impact. I am keen that he understands our situation because, when he does, I think he may have some very interesting ideas – and maybe even some interesting expertise for us to consider.

On the other hand we could play it by ear, hope we get lucky and find something we have in common with the client.

Chapter 4 **PACES: Understanding the Prospective Client**

AC BEFORE ES - A COMMONSENSE FRAMEWORK

Imagine visiting a chiropodist because the arch of your foot is causing pain. You begin to explain the problem to the chiropodist who seems to listen for a short while and then begins to take his shoes off. 'I had that sort of problem once' he says, 'and then I got these shoes. They're really great. Here, try them on. You can keep them. I've got a couple more pairs exactly the same at home.'

Dubiously you try the shoes on. They quite simply do not fit. 'I don't think these will help' you say. 'Try walking in them, give them a go' replies the chiropodist. You do. They are simply no use whatsoever. The pain in the arch is reduced due to the increased discomfort everywhere else. 'This is simply not the solution' you say. 'Think positively' replies the chiropodist. 'They positively aren't going to help' you find yourself saying.

You hand the shoes back to the chiropodist and decide to leave. As you are walking out of the door you hear the chiropodist mumbling about clients who won't listen and who don't know what's really good for them.

I guess you would not have very much faith in an 'expert' who behaved in such a way. That chiropodist would not have very many patients. Yet it is this sort of behaviour which professionals demonstrate time and time again when they are given the opportunity to engage in a selling meeting. We have observed this countless times in both real life and in role play.

Quite clearly the professional needs to fully understand the prospective client, her business, the business environment, the plans the business has for the future, how it plans to achieve its future objectives, and the risks, opportunities and issues it faces in going forward before coming up with services and solutions which are meant to 'help' the client organisation.

Our observations are corroborated by other notable writers in the field of selling professional services. Richard K. Carlson in his book *Personal Selling Strategies for Consultants and Professionals* states the following:

"The most common and the most damaging consultant behaviour that I have observed is the tendency to jump at any opportunity to offer a solution".

"When you offer a premature solution:

>You have a good chance of being wrong.

>You may not get the opportunity to come up with another solution".

So why is it that professionals so often make such a fundamental error in their selling approach? After all, the PACES model is extremely simple. It requires no great intellectual capability to understand. The 'A' of the model (ascertain) comes before the 'E' (explain). The model suggests that we ascertain the client's situation and requirements before we explore and explain a suitable way forward. First understand the problem in detail, then devise a solution. Don't try to come up with solutions before we understand the problem.

WHY PACES 'GOES WRONG'

Professionals themselves have provided the answers to us. Among the explanations we have heard are:

Explanation 1

'In a selling meeting we are expected to sell.' When asked the question, 'Who expects you to sell?' we get differing replies. These vary from:

1. 'Our organisation - we have new business development objectives to hit and we need to take every opportunity to sell our services.'

2. 'The client - the client wants to hear what you have got and what you can do to help.'

3. 'Me - if I see an opportunity I'm not going to let it go by.'

The common thread among all these replies is that there is a misunderstanding about what selling is. These professionals believe that selling is about talking. Talking is a part of selling but talking about the wrong things is a sure way to turn a prospective client into a client for one of our competitors.

Remember the chiropodist - perhaps he thought that his job was to sell.

Explanation 2

Another commonly heard explanation goes as follows: 'When you hear a client talk about a problem you can help them with, you naturally tell them then and there. You can't just sit and nod.'

In a well-tested simulation of a first meeting a conversation went like this:

Client   One of the things I want to get under way is our CDQ - Customer Driven Quality - programme. This has not been driven forward in the UK and we can make big improvements if we get it going.

Professional Well we can probably help you there. We have experts in this field and we have supported many of our clients helping them to gain ISO9000 accreditation. I am sure we could also help you.

Client	No, we already have ISO9000. CDQ is an internal process. It's really about making the company totally client-focused.
Professional	Again we have expertise in this. We have worked with many major manufacturers like your company and helped them to devise and institute customer service programmes.
Client	Well it's really a bit more than a customer service programme. It begins by firstly developing the internal processes, ensuring that they are robust and are fully aligned with delivering ultimate customer satisfaction.
Professional	Oh, so it involves re-engineering some of your processes?
Client	I guess you could call it that.
Professional	Well we definitely can help. In addition to our expertise in ISO9000 and customer service development we do a lot of work in Business Process Re-engineering. Would you like to talk with one of our specialists in this area? I'm sure he could give you a lot of ideas.
Client	Well possibly he could - but my first priority is to recruit someone to take charge of the CDQ programme.
Professional	Do you have someone in mind?
Client	No, I'm going to have to go outside for this appointment.
Professional	We have an executive recruitment arm that could do this for you. They have an excellent track record in finding top people and I know they have recruited individuals in the service and quality fields.
Client	I've already got our personnel people working on this one. They are very good and I always use internal resources first time round when I'm looking to recruit. I've only ever used recruitment consultants when we've drawn a blank ourselves, and I have to say my experiences then weren't very favourable.

At this stage if the client begins to complain about his foot and his painful arch we can be fairly certain that the professional will begin to untie his shoelaces.

As Carlson says:

> "…professionals - who may begin a sales interview by asking questions intended to uncover needs - often become side-tracked. As soon as the prospect mentions something for which they have a solution, they snap at the bait and begin describing what they can do, usually in terms of 'Here's what we've done in situations similar to yours.' Not only do these people present a solution prematurely, but they deter the prospect from telling them more about their needs".

Explanation 3

A third reason given by some professionals being totally honest about first meetings, goes something along the following lines: 'When we're talking about his business there are many times when I'm on shaky ground. I like it when I can get the conversation onto something that I know about.'

A very honest explanation - but one which clearly has nothing to do with good selling practice. We may be very interested in a particular area of expertise. We may be very knowledgeable in our subject. However, if it has no apparent relevance to the prospective client, then it is of little value.

Most professionals we have ever worked with tell us that they do not want to be trained to become 'high pressure salesmen'. Yet the epitome of a high pressure salesman is the person who talks about his product and tries to sell his product to an unwilling customer. Unwittingly the untrained professional can demonstrate the very behaviours he or she would most seek to avoid.

The worst outcome from this type of behaviour results when the prospect reacts badly to being sold to. The prospect may start to raise objection after objection, she may even become personally objectionable. After the initial meeting she may become strangely unobtainable. The untrained professional can then draw the conclusion that 'selling' does not suit the professional arena and future 'selling' meetings develop into an apparently aimless and unstructured 'chat' where the main aim of the professional appears to be to do everything possible to avoid being seen to 'sell'.

HOW TO ASCERTAIN THE PROSPECTIVE CLIENT'S SITUATION AND REQUIREMENTS AND HOW TO CONFIRM YOUR UNDERSTANDING

To master the 'A' and the 'C' of the PACES process the professional needs to do three things well. He needs to:

1. Ask questions in the most effective manner.

2. Demonstrate that he can take the discussion logically forward by having listened and responded to what the client has said.

3. Choose the right questions for an effective 'Funnel' process.

The Funnel Process

A useful model which guides us through the first two of these three skill areas is the Funnel. The funnel is shown in Figure 4.1. You will see that the funnel process takes us smoothly from the 'A' (ascertaining the client's situation and requirements) into the 'C' of the PACES model (confirming our understanding of the client's situation and requirements).

Figure 4.1: The funnel process

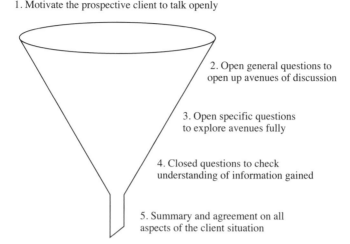

1. Motivate the prospective client to talk openly

2. Open general questions to open up avenues of discussion

3. Open specific questions to explore avenues fully

4. Closed questions to check understanding of information gained

5. Summary and agreement on all aspects of the client situation

The funnel works as follows:

1. We motivate the prospective client to talk openly and answer our questions

On scores of occasions we have seen professionals fail to get useful and detailed information from prospective clients even though they have prepared the questions they plan to ask and even though they use these prepared questions in the meeting. This can be very frustrating to the planned professional. One of the main reasons why the prospective client may not be forthcoming is explained as follows.

The professional knows he needs to ask questions very early in the meeting in order to identify needs and wants. He therefore prepares his questions and, as soon in the meeting as he can, he begins to bombard the client with his information-seeking 'missiles'.

The whole process is driven by what the professional wants and what the professional sees as being the 'logical' conduct and structure of the meeting. The client is not considered in the planning process.

Within minutes of the meeting starting, the client is being hit by questions, some of them in potentially sensitive areas, and she is typically thinking:

"Why does he need this information?" or,

"Where are we going with this?" or,

"I thought he said on the phone he wanted to come and talk about some ideas his firm had, how come he's just asking me for information?"

Sometimes it is patently clear from the expression on the prospective client's face that she is not comfortable with being questioned.

Often the questioning is interrupted by the client interjecting with something along the lines of,

> "You said that your firm had expertise and ideas in this area. I think we've talked enough about my company. I'd like to know now what you can do for us."

The professional has gained very little useful data up to this point. The answers which have been elicited have been brief to the point of being begrudging and now he is faced with the prospect of talking about his firm's services or capabilities without having any real understanding as to their applicability to the client to whom he is talking.

Most times this can be totally avoided by the use of an introduction such as the one shown in the last chapter and specifically including a link similar to the one used there:

> "Good. As I mentioned earlier, we recognise that every organisation is unique so, rather than, at this stage, going into more detail of what we do and how we do it, some of which I believe would be very relevant to you and some that would be less so, I would value the opportunity of finding out more about your organisation so that towards the end of the meeting, and perhaps beyond, we can focus on those things that would be of most interest to you. How does that sound?"

It is used before any questions are asked and is designed to explain to the prospective client why it is valuable for them to spend time answering questions and giving information.

Given such an explanation the prospective client understands the reason for the questions and can see a potential benefit in sharing information. We cannot remember a situation we have seen where a professional has used a powerful and well expressed introduction and has not been allowed to explore with questions.

This can be likened to putting a pound coin in a parking meter. It buys you time - in this case, questioning time.

2. Start with open general questions

Most people have come across the concept of open and closed questions. It is considered by many to be 'old hat'. Training in questioning occurs (suitably) in many types of courses. Despite the intellectual simplicity of the concept it is surprising how superficial some understanding is.

Trainer to group	Have we come across the concept of open and closed questions before?
Response	Nods all round.
Trainer	OK, can someone tell me the difference between an open and a closed question?
Response	Yes, an open question is one which gives you a long answer. People can't answer it 'Yes' or 'No'.
Trainer	Right, but how would I know if I was looking at an open or a closed question? What would indicate this?

Response	Silence.
Trainer	I mean, if I looked at two questions written side by side, one open and one closed, what would be the structural difference?
Response	Silence.

Perhaps as the reader you know the answer. It is obvious. However, we have met many groups and individuals who profess to have been trained in questioning and who have 'temporarily forgotten' that the essential difference between an open question and a closed question is that an open question must begin with one of these words - Who, What, Where, How, Why, When or Which or requests such as Please tell me... or Could you please describe... If the question begins in any other way it is, by definition, a closed question and could be answered with one word - either 'Yes' or 'No'.

Why people tend to ask closed questions

Despite protestations by many, our observations over the years prove that most people have poor ability in asking open questions. There are a number of explanations suggested as to why this is so. Among these are:

Explanation 1

It is easier to ask a closed question. This is undoubtedly so.

Explanation 2

It has been noted for years that very young children have the ability to ask very open questions. Those of us who have had children will recall the sometimes unending question 'Why?' It is as if a young child's brain is like blotting paper - it wants to absorb as much as it can. However, as children start to develop an understanding of their world, their questioning changes.

Instead of 'Why?' the question becomes, 'Why does it do that, Dad? Is it because...?' The child is trying to see if the answer fits into its model of the world. The most comfortable answer is one in which the parent replies in some way to the affirmative.

Most closed questions indicate very clearly the line of response which the questioner would feel most comfortable in receiving. However, such questions are extremely limited as a means of information gathering and do very little to help us to really understand the other person and their position.

Explanation 3

Explanation 3 is sometimes expressed in the following way:

'All this stuff about open and closed questions is theoretical. Most of the time you ask a closed question people tell you a lot more than "Yes" or "No". In fact I know people whom I have a hard time shutting up no matter what sort of question I ask them! I don't see the point in practising all this open questioning stuff.'

This is a weak excuse - usually given after observation has proven that the individual concerned rarely asks open questions.

Of course there are people who will talk no matter what the question. Equally there are other people who are more reticent and who have to be asked the sorts of questions which will encourage them to 'open up'. The individual who continuously uses only closed questions will not fare very well in opening up others who have to be 'drawn'.

The argument that closed questions work as well as open questions is like a golfer saying he does not practise with his sand wedge as he never gets into a bunker. All golfers would like to think this could be the case but the reality is that in difficult situations one needs expertise with all of the clubs in the bag. Not all golf is played on the greens and not all clients are loquacious.

The difference between open general and open specific questions

Step 2 of the Funnel process says to begin with open general questions and Step 3 then goes on to say that we follow up with open specific questions. So what is the difference between an open general and an open specific question?

Initially the two question types look very similar. Both open general and open specific questions begin with the 'W' words - Who, What, Why, Where, When, How and Which.

However, an open general question will usually give a response which is uninfluenced by the question which is being asked. An open specific question will receive an answer which will have been more influenced by the question.

For example, two questions which could form part of a meeting designed to get to understand a client's business and its production processes could be:

'What effects have the new packaging regulations had on your business?'

'What problems have the new packaging regulations caused for your business?'

There is a subtle but significant difference in the questions. The first question has a far wider scope. The question seeks to understand what effects - good, bad and indifferent - the regulations have had. The second question only concerns itself with the negative aspects - the problems. The person answering the question is led to talk about problems.

Over the years we have had people argue that the second question is the more effective. After all, they claim, the professional is in the meeting to find out what the problems are and to provide solutions. The unfortunate reality is that a client knows when she has been asked a leading question - and can choose to react accordingly.

There does not need to be a debate as to which question is better - in a good meeting probably both will be used. However, there is a best order for using the two questions.

The first question - the more open of the two - should be used first. This is for two reasons. Firstly it is less likely to create a defensive reaction from the client. This is because there is less vested interest (i.e. 'problems') in the question. Secondly the question is more likely to provide a wider information trawl.

Imagine the meeting:

Professional   What effects have the new packaging regulations had on your business?

Client	Well they forced us to look hard at how we packaged all of our lines. It was something we hadn't done seriously for years. We decided that we should take a genuinely creative look at our packaging. We used experts from both in house and outside to come up with ideas, and in the next few months we will be launching some exciting new lines utilising innovative packaging processes.

On the surface of it, this response may not seem like good news to the professional - but it is the *real* picture. The professional needs to keep exploring (funnelling) - understanding more and more of the picture. At an appropriate time in the meeting he may be able to come back with:

Professional	You have said that the new packaging, whilst very attractive, is less regular in shape than the old traditional lines; what problems does that bring you?

The 'problems' question (in which the professional may have a vested interest) is now positioned differently. It has been asked in context and it has been asked in an informed way - based on the knowledge which the client has given to the professional in the preceding part of the meeting.

Again, our observations over the years demonstrate that even when people do ask open questions, the majority are open specific questions and are leading at too early a stage in the meeting. It seems we can't resist asking questions which tell the other person how we want them to answer. Unfortunately most people resist strongly being led by questions - to the point that some will even lie in order to provide their questioner with an answer he does not want to hear!

Open specific questions have a very important function in any meeting. They are the sort of questions which are most likely to give substance to the opportunities, issues and problems which will provide a professional with work. We must just make sure that they are used at the appropriate time. As in courtship, the ardent suitor may want to get down to the kissing and cuddling as soon as possible. However, courtship requires a period of getting to know you and hand-holding may need to precede any more intimate contact.

Going in for the early 'kill' with leading questions is a sure way to raise client resistance and cause the client to mistrust our motives.

Can one, therefore, classify questions as either open general or open specific? Every person we have seen attempting this has ended up in an intellectual debate with people trying to prove that his open general question is really somewhat specific. The answer is that all open questions live somewhere on a continuum stretching from totally open and general at one end to open but extremely leading at the other. (See Figure 4.2.)

Figure 4.2: The open question continuum

Totally general questions   Totally specific questions

The one guideline which can be applied with some degree of accuracy is that a very open and general question will usually be short and contain very few words whereas a question (almost by definition) becomes more specific as it becomes longer.

In the funnelling process the aim is to start the discussion on any subject (funnel) with some good open general questions and then to listen to what is said (and not said) and to follow up with other open questions based on the picture which is being built up. As we seek to define more detail in the picture, the questions have to become more specific and so the skilled practitioner 'naturally' makes the conversion from asking open general questions to open specific questions. Closed questions will also be used in the information-gathering part of the meeting where we are tying down details.

Encouraging open responses through good listening

A good meeting in which we are ascertaining the prospective client's situation and requirements should not appear to the client as a question and answer session. A good meeting should seem more like a logical free-flowing discussion - but with the client doing most of the talking. In order to achieve this the professional must move the meeting along based on the responses to the questions which he asks. This can only be achieved if the professional has actually listened to the answers which the client has provided. More importantly, the professional must demonstrate to the other person that they are really listening. It matters not a jot that we have total recall of everything which is said in a meeting if it appears to the other person that we are not showing interest during the meeting itself. If we appear not to be paying close attention, people will very quickly cease to give us information.

We must therefore have the ability both to really understand what the other person is saying and 'where they are coming from' and also to demonstrate this. The way in which this is achieved is simply through listening. The word 'simply' is a misnomer. For many of us proficiency in this skill is far from simple. Demonstrating that we are listening takes a number of forms which range from being quite passive to the point where we demonstrate active listening.

Demonstrating our listening

Staying quiet – allowing the client space to talk

This is the most passive way of showing we are prepared to listen. We simply let the other person talk and do not attempt to interrupt them. Simple as it may seem there are some who find this difficult. The old adage goes, 'Some people listen, others wait to talk.' When we meet people who wait to talk it becomes very evident quite quickly. These people always seem a little distant when we are talking to them as they are really in the process of forming their response rather than listening to what we have to say.

Using positive body language

There are signs which indicate that we are listening. Conversely there are signs which indicate that we are not. A good listener will deliberately manifest signs that she is listening. A posture of slightly leaning forward, head turned a shade to one side (turning one ear toward the speaker), good eye contact and appropriately timed nodding of the head in understanding, give the speaker the clear feedback that his spoken message is being paid close attention.

We have never met anyone who told us that they deliberately used negative, discouraging body language - so is there any point in mentioning the subject? The fact that no one deliberately uses 'non-listening' body language does not mean that it is not used. Most people in most meetings are unaware of their body language. It is unfortunately common to see people displaying 'neutral' (at best) body language in meetings with clients.

Video tapes of role-plays also bear out this conclusion. The person who really looks as though she is interested is one step ahead of the person who hasn't got a clue how she looks to the prospective client.

The message is clear. Demonstrate positive, listening body language and do it consciously.

Using encouraging words, phrases and 'noises'

We are all familiar with these devices. They are words like 'Really?' - said with the inflection of the voice being raised at the end of the word - and phrases like 'Go on!' 'Uh huh', and 'Mmmmm' are two examples which fall into the 'noises' category.

Such expressions are usually accompanied by raised eyebrows, a widening of the eyes and other positive body language indicators which are all saying to the speaker, 'I am listening. I am interested. I want to hear more of what you have to say.'

Whilst we are all familiar with these devices some people get more value from them because they employ them more often. It is hard to overuse this simple device unless one develops a clichéd approach. Using 'You don't say' ten times in a row could cause the speaker to retort with, 'Yes, I do say!'

The key is to vary the expression.

Taking notes

Taking notes in business meetings is quite the accepted norm. The person who fails to take notes is the odd person out today and we have often heard people remark negatively about another person who has participated in a detailed meeting and not taken one note throughout. The excuses are as plausible as they are predictable.

> 'I wanted to give the meeting my full attention and I can't write and listen.'

> 'If you're writing notes you can't maintain eye contact. It appears that you're more interested in writing than listening.'

People who make such remarks are either poor note-takers or are not really interested in what the other person has to say, despite protestations to the contrary. As note-taking is an accepted demonstration of paying attention it is up to us to learn how to carry out this function. We dress smartly for business meetings as this is the socially accepted thing to do. Similarly we need to be able to perform the socially accepted skill of note-taking.

Note-taking does not mean taking down everything which is said verbatim. A good note-taker will jot down the significant details emerging from a meeting into a format which he or she will be able to use after the meeting has finished. Like any skill it needs practice and with practice it will develop into a good habit.

Unbundling key words and phrases

We have had people in the past tell us that all of the above ways of demonstrating listening can be faked. Nod, look interested, scribble a few things onto a piece of paper

and say, 'That's interesting' a few times and you have it made. We would suggest that
this is a rather dangerous strategy and that people are observant enough to realise the fake
from the genuine article.

However, unbundling is not something which can be faked. Unbundling can only be
carried out by someone who is paying attention, listening closely and trying to genuinely
understand what the other person is trying to communicate.

It could go something like this:

Client	We have developed our forecasting systems so that shortfalls or overstocking are not usually a problem.
Professional	Usually?
Client	Yes, 85 to 90 per cent of our orders are for existing products. Where we do sometimes have a hiccup is with new products.
Professional	New products?
Client	Our traditional lines have been emulated by many of our competitors and therefore to stay ahead we are increasingly having to develop new product ranges.
Professional	From what you're saying then, even though the problem is not great now, it is likely to grow?
Client	Probably - unless we can find ways of predicting the volumes of these new lines more accurately.

What started out as an unpromising line from the client has turned into a potential need on
which the professional may be able to offer assistance. The opportunity occurred because
the professional was listening very closely to what the client said.

There is no reason why a person we are talking with for the first time should trust us to the
point where they will tell us everything. We totally unburden ourselves only to those people in
whom we choose to trust. However, there are often words which people will use which may
seem insignificant in themselves but which may be the tip of a very important iceberg.

'We are quite satisfied' could mean that there are a number of aspects about
which we are not happy.

'We will not pursue the subject at this point in time' could mean that there is
a date at which the subject will be reviewed.

'There is considerable opinion that we should take this next step' could mean
that there are some significant voices in opposition who are not yet convinced.

So often such words and expressions pass us by. We decide they are not particularly
significant or meaningful and do not explore by unbundling.

The professional who is a good unbundler demonstrates very markedly that he is determined
to really understand - not to just understand the position from a superficial point of view.
Unbundling produces a virtuous circle. By unbundling we demonstrate that we want to
understand. By demonstrating that we want to understand, the client will be motivated to be

more forthcoming in the detail of the information which she chooses to share with us.

Another significant reason for unbundling is that some people do not explain themselves clearly at all times.

For example:

Professional	You described earlier the main objectives your organisation has for the future. How will you go about achieving these objectives?
Client	Well, we haven't exactly been sitting on our hands, you know. We have already done a lot of work and we are quite a way down the road with a number of projects related to improving our marketing tools. Do you know what I mean?

The temptation is to say, 'Yes I know what you mean - of course!' We fear appearing stupid if we reply to the effect that we don't understand. However, what the client has said is not clear at all. If she was talking to a person within her own organisation that other person would probably know what she meant by 'marketing tools', would probably know how many projects there were and what they were about and may even know how far 'down the road' they were.

The professional must begin to unpick and unbundle.

Professional	Broadly speaking, yes... but I am not totally clear on what you include as 'marketing tools' in your particular company. What are these?

Unbundling is a skill demonstrated by a good listener - but this does not yet qualify us to claim to be an active listener.

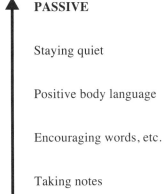

PASSIVE

Staying quiet

Positive body language

Encouraging words, etc.

Taking notes

Unbundling

Summarising

Reflecting

ACTIVE

Active listening

The fifth stage of the funnel process is to summarise and reflect. This is the demonstration of Active Listening. An active listener not only demonstrates all of the previous listening skills, he is able to give feedback through summarising the facts and content of the messages spoken by the client and reflecting on any feelings which may have been associated with the message.

Summarising

A question we have been asked innumerable times over the years is:

> 'How do I know when I've reached the bottom of a funnel? I explore a subject with a client and when I think I understand I leave it and move on to something else. A bit later on in the meeting it becomes evident that there is more I needed to know about the first subject and I have to jump back to it. The meeting gets really messy and unstructured.'

This type of problem is one we witness almost daily. The resultant 'mess' we term 'funnel hopping' - jumping from subject to subject in an almost random way. The remedy is to carry out the fourth and fifth parts of the funnel process. When we believe we are at the bottom of a funnel (i.e. we believe that we have the full picture) we should check our understanding. A number of immense benefits emanate from this practice. These are:

- Having to summarise really does make us work to understand what the client has been saying

- The act of summarising often causes us to realise that we cannot complete the summary because we lack certain information - hence another question is prompted

- We eliminate errors and misunderstandings because the other person will correct these. These misunderstandings may or may not be our 'fault'. It could be that the client has expressed herself poorly or in an incomplete manner. Fault is of no consequence to the summary. All we are attempting to do is to ensure that our understanding of the information is the same as that which the client has been trying to communicate

- We give the client a powerful demonstration that we are listening and are making every attempt to understand what she has to say

- If our summary is incomplete the client will usually fill in the gaps and add more information - enabling us to more adequately finish off a funnel

A complaint which is voiced of some clients is:

> 'He keeps repeating himself. I understand first time round but he feels he has to tell me another four times.'

If you have this problem with some people, try using a summary after they have imparted information to you. In this way they will know that you understand rather than being unsure and feeling that repetition will reinforce their message.

There is some misunderstanding about summarising. We have observed people who were told they were good at summarising because after an hour's meeting they spent 30 seconds at the end summarising the agreements of the discussion and the way forward. Whilst this is good practice this is not the summarising associated with active listening. Nor, after speaking about her accounting process for 20 minutes is the professional's 'summary' of the client's processes amounting to, 'So, all in all, it works pretty well then.'

Whilst a summary should not be a parrot-fashion repetition of what has been said, it must contain an accurate interpretation ('picture') of the key facts - demonstrating that the information has been heard, interpreted and stored reasonably accurately.

Every meeting will be different but a good active listener will summarise every five or ten minutes - and sometimes more often than this.

Reflecting

Few people speak for any length of time using purely informational language. By that we mean language where the words alone convey the entirety of the message. If we did, we would come across as a bit robotic or like an announcement on a public address system. Because we are human beings, we tend to communicate using words, tone of voice and body language. We are also wired to pick up on this fuller range of communications naturally.

In particular, if someone is talking about their feelings, we might notice physical and auditory changes that support this. If someone is passionate about what they are saying, their voice might get more animated, and their body language more upright or dynamic.

Likewise if someone says something positive but their body language and tone of voice do not support the words, they might appear 'incongruent', and it is mostly through their non-verbal communication that we sense this.

Good active listening recognises this. If we reflect back to the speaker - using words to acknowledge the emotion we have sensed - we are demonstrating more fully that we have really understood and that we know 'where the other person is coming from'.

For example:

'You are obviously very passionate about this project...'

'I sense that you are slightly apprehensive about the next step...'

'I get the impression that even though you were angry, there is also a touch of sadness...'

'Clearly you are enthusiastic about this...'

Passion, apprehension, anger, sadness and enthusiasm are examples of emotions that may come across as part of the message. Reflecting tells the other person that we recognise how they feel about the subject in question.

In talking with professionals over the years and asking them what they hope to achieve in early meetings with clients it is common to hear the objective, 'I try to sell myself first'. When asked, 'So how do you achieve this?' a typical reply is, 'I try to build rapport and empathy with the customer.' When further pursued with the question, 'So how do you actually build rapport and empathy?' the quality of answers usually erodes rapidly into comments about finding out what sports the other person is interested in and talking about that.

We once saw empathy well described as:

> 'Putting yourself in another's shoes without wanting to wear them.'

Dedicating the concentration and effort to really try to understand how the other person feels, to the point of verbalising this, is the most effective way of demonstrating to a prospective client that you really want to build empathy, rapport and trust.

Active listening proficiency

So how good is the average professional as an active listener?

Whilst clearly there are exceptions, the average is somewhere between mediocre and poor. (As an exercise write down a list including the names of all the really good listeners in your organisation. If the list is short reflect on the fact that your organisation is probably a consulting/advisory firm and that great listening should be a core competency regardless of how vital it is to the success of any selling efforts. Perhaps also reflect on whether you would appear on such a list if it was compiled by your colleagues!)

Perhaps we should not be surprised. During our early lives we are taught all of the communication skills - bar one. We are taught by our parents how to talk, we are taught how to read and write. Most people who participate in our training courses, however, have never had any lessons or training in listening skills. Being told to listen in class and being punished for not doing so hardly counts as a lesson in communication skills in our assessment.

People who express themselves well using the spoken or written word do so because they work hard at the proficiencies of these media. They study and they practise and they combine this skills development with whatever natural talent they are fortunate enough to possess. Proficient speed-readers do the same. To become proficient listeners we need the motivation to want to be well above the mediocre. With the motivation in place we stand some chance of devoting the effort and energy into achieving a communication ability possessed by all too few.

Active Listening - a Case Study

The power of active listening was once demonstrated to us by a colleague with whom we worked in a previous company. Mark had been responsible for co-ordinating the training of a group of senior managers from the European subsidiaries of a large US high-tech company. The training had gone very well and the MD of the UK company told Mark he was so convinced that he wanted to use us to carry out work in the UK. The MD (as was his wont) made this decision without consulting his three senior divisional sales managers. They were told after the decision had been made and were given a fait accompli.

I was appointed as the consultant for the UK group and the day arrived when we had to carry out our first research into the UK client company. I picked up Mark in the morning and as we drove to the client's HQ he expressed his concern that the divisional sales managers might be somewhat hostile toward us due to the autocratic way in which the project had been decided.

As Mark had all of the connections and knowledge of the client organisation, it was agreed that he would take the lead in the three meetings we had scheduled (one with each of the sales managers). I would take a fairly low-key role.

The first meeting was at 10 o'clock. The atmosphere was almost icy. My colleague sat opposite the sales manager who was jacketed and in position behind his large desk. I sat slightly behind and to one side of Mark. It would have been easy for Mark to hide behind the MD's decision and to take the line that it was a fait accompli for us all therefore we had better just get on with it. He didn't. He made every effort to really listen to what the first sales manager had to say. He demonstrated this through active listening. He summarised regularly to make sure that he had understood and to demonstrate that he wanted to understand.

From time to time he reflected the feelings and concerns of the sales manager - demonstrating that he understood how the sales manager felt about the various subjects we discussed. Expressions such as 'So how you see it is...' and 'So your feelings are...' were a regular feature of the meeting.

After about 30 minutes the atmosphere had changed significantly. Mark and the sales manager were physically closer together. The sales manager drew diagrams and small charts on his pad to explain things which Mark was clearly interested in. Mark had to move into such a position that he could see. The sales manager was by this stage quite comfortable with this. The body language which had started as rather formal and stilted became more expansive and relaxed.

At the end of an hour and a half there had clearly been a meeting of minds and one opponent was now open to our involvement - if not yet an advocate.

The second meeting was a re-run of the first. A defensive and totally unconvinced person at the start was 'converted' over the next 90 minutes.

We had lunch and Mark and I met with the third of the sales managers. Though not quite as 'stiff' as his other two colleagues, he would have proven a tough nut for most people. The 'magic' of active listening worked again. In the late afternoon we were on our way back down the motorway with the UK client's most influential people supporting the training which their people were to receive and believing that those who were going to carry it out really understood what was needed and why.

After a few minutes in the car I turned to Mark and asked him a question. He did not reply. The reason was simple. He was asleep. He was mentally exhausted from the three meetings. For the best part of five hours he had turned up his active listening skills to a very high pitch. That requires motivation, effort and mental stamina.

A scarce skill

Almost everyone who understands what active listening is, wants to become good at it. However, few people work on developing it to any level of proficiency. We may be wrong but we believe that one reason why really good active listening is such a scarce skill is that it does require such a lot of mental energy. It is all to easy to nod and say, 'Yeah, I understand.'

The rarest and finest of skills all take work to master. It is only by application and practice that we will improve. A theoretical understanding of the skill is only the beginning.

Most importantly the benefits of active listening will only be fully delivered if we approach the skill as one which is designed to help us help others. If we see active listening as a technique to enable us to manipulate and gain advantage we should not be surprised if people 'spot the technique' and see us as behaving in an unnatural and false way. Instead of building empathy and trust, the application of the skills as a pure technique will erode the very things we seek to build.

CHOOSING QUESTIONS FOR AN EFFECTIVE FUNNEL PROCESS

The 'Business' funnels

If we are to sell a service or capability which we claim will benefit the client's organisation, it is imperative that we first of all understand the client's business. Whilst decision-makers may have personal agendas which affect their decisions (something we will address further in Section Four) any decision to use professional advice has to be justified to shareholders and employees on rational, logical grounds. Therefore clients are not going to invest in buying services which fail to add value to their specific business.

Very early in the meeting we must find out where the prospective client's business is today and where it has come from in the past. Most importantly however, we must ascertain where the business is heading in the future. We cannot repair the problems of yesterday, and the problems and opportunities of today are probably already being addressed. Where opportunity is most likely to lie is in the unfulfilled opportunities, unresolved problems and unaddressed issues which are on the horizon.

Questions about the business can be asked in three tenses - past, present and future. It is an established fact that the individuals who are most successful at selling ask more of their questions in the future tense. Obvious, when one thinks about it!

For the future a prospective client may want to:

- Be more cost-effective

- Be more timely in responding to its customers

- Increase its business volumes

- Reduce its working capital

- Make more qualified decisions

- Be more competitive in its current place

- Portray a better image

- Reduce staff turnover

- Attract the best people in the marketplace

- Reduce time to market

- Comply with impending legislation

These are examples of business issues. Prospective clients have two ways of addressing these types of issue. Firstly they can deal with them utilising their own resources. Alternatively they can employ outside expertise. However, we cannot fully understand the issue, the size of the issue and its potential impact if we do not firstly understand where these issues lie in relation to the future direction of the business.

For instance, reducing time to market for new products may be an issue for a prospective client company. How significant an issue it will be, will be determined by factors such as:

- How demanding the market will be for new products

- The types of customers the company will be supplying in the future

- The numbers of new products which the company is likely to have to produce in the future

- The likely responsiveness of future competitors

- The plans which the company already has in place to shorten time to market

The professional needs to understand this market and company background as early as possible. Whilst a professional may be a market specialist and therefore have a good grasp of the market situation, what he does not know is the prospective client's:

- Perception of the market

- Business

- Perception of her own business

The third factor is extremely important. No study of information and no amount of planning can determine the individual client's perception. The professional with all of the statistics in the world at his fingertips can approach a prospective client who he knows is falling behind the game in terms of (by way of example) time to market. However, if the perception of the individuals within this organisation is that this is not an important issue then he will struggle to convince them that this is so.

People within the prospective client organisation may argue that the perceived wisdom of the pundits is invalid because:

- They suffer from management myopia. They can see, touch and feel past and current successes but have no processes for envisioning a different future

- There may be a series of even bigger problems which may need more urgent resolution

- The time-to-market issue may in itself only be a symptom of a bigger problem

- Management may have plans in place to resolve the problem

Research information is always out of date. The only question is how far out of date it is.

The conclusion we draw again is that the only way to really understand the perceived business issues and the positioning of these issues is to ask the key individuals within the prospective client organisation.

In numerous surveys carried out with business customers into their attitudes towards suppliers, the biggest shortcoming of salespeople has been summed up by customers as:

'They don't understand my business.'

The perception of the salespeople invariably differs in this respect. However, salespeople don't make the buying decisions and they don't sign the cheques. The perception of the customer, or client, is the only important perception. Providers of professional services are under an even greater obligation by the very nature of their offering to really understand the client, how the business operates and where it is going in the future. In a competitive marketplace we cannot afford to run the risk of being accused of not understanding our clients' businesses.

We cannot plan every question which we will ask in an exploratory early meeting. However, we can plan the broad subjects into which we would wish to delve. In other words we can plan the 'funnel opening' questions - the open general questions which start the free flow of information.

Some examples of funnel opening questions which could be asked

- How is your company positioned today?
- What are your key business objectives in the foreseeable future?
- What are the main strategies that you will employ to achieve these objectives?
- What is your current organisational structure?
- What impact will your strategies have on the size and shape of your organisation?
- What are the biggest pressures in your market today?
- What will be the issues in your marketplace in the future?
- What plans do you have to increase your competitiveness in the future?
- What are the likely changes you are going to have to face in the future?
- What are the issues for your organisation in dealing with future changes?
- In the light of your future strategy, what path or strategy are you considering for:
  - IT?
  - Manpower?
  - Financial management?
  - Sales?
  - Marketing?
  - Taxation issues?
  - Distribution?
  - Product development?
  - R & D?
  - (name your own subject area)

For the professional in IT or marketing - or any other expertise area - the final question is the one we want to hear answered. This is the one where there may be opportunity and work. Whilst there is no specific order in which these example funnel openers should be posed, we would recommend that the 'self-interest' question at the bottom is definitely the last of these types of questions to be asked. By the time we have explored all of the preceding funnels we should be developing a clear understanding of the client's perception of the future of her organisation and where the gaps and opportunities lie.

Another valid reason for taking the discussion down this route is the often-quoted observation that people love to talk about their businesses and they like to talk on their agenda. We feel less comfortable - and sometimes manipulated - when people want to get onto their agenda straight away. In following the suggested route the professional is demonstrating interest in the client - a step toward establishing compatibility and ultimately building a feeling of trust.

One word of caution. While we may be keen to explore the client's business before finding out about potential opportunities, sometimes the client will feel an urgent need to inform us of an opportunity or issue her organisation is facing. If this were the case she could be frustrated by our determination to structure the meeting in a particular way. The key message is to follow the client's agenda as closely as possible so, in this situation, we should funnel this particular issue/opportunity until we can demonstrate a real understanding of it in all its detail. The key then is to motivate the client 'back' to a conversation about her business (the business funnels) so that we can "understand the context within which this particular issue/opportunity exists".

Demonstrating competence through questions

David Maister in his article 'How Clients Choose' writes:

> "I discount all your assertions about your expertise until you give me some evidence to back them up. For example don't tell me about your experience in my industry (or on a particular topic). Rather, illustrate it by asking questions that reveal your knowledge of key industry terminology, facts and latest figures or latest events. That way, I'll draw my own conclusions (which I'm going to do anyway) about how well you understand my business and my issues".

The examples of funnel openers in the previous section are deliberately written in an open general style. This is mainly for simplicity. From time to time we have had people protest about the format of these questions. Their main point is that the questions may sound extremely naive to the potential client - particularly if the meeting was positioned with the professional being some kind of industry specialist. The comments are valid. However, we must take care not to lose the value of a question which is open and as wide-scoping as possible.

When finding out about a prospective client's business it is important to preface some questions with *competence builders*.

If talking with a prospect in the banking sector a question you may wish to ask could be:

'What do you see as the main issues impacting on your business today and in the future?'

This may better be expressed as:

'A number of our clients are finding that with the upturn in the economy there appears to be an increasing focus on increasing the asset base. Clearly this puts pressures into the market and drives down margins. That is one issue we're seeing but I'd be interested to know what you see as the main factors impacting upon your business today and into the future?'

The prefix sentences imply that we know about her industry - without any attempt to air our 'expert opinion'. At the end of the question the prospect is left to express her own thoughts.

Another example - this time the prospect is a £35 million turnover computer systems integrator.

'The industry has had for many years to live with slim margins on hardware - and software is also moving rapidly to being a commodity offering.

What plans do you have for your company given these difficult market conditions?'

This question illustrates more competence than:

'What plans do you have for the future?'

Competence builders must preface the question - not be added as a suffix. There is a great danger that a wrongly expressed question:

- Turns into an example of the professional trying to impress with his knowledge instead of trying to seek information from the prospective client
- Is seen by the client as a deliberate attempt to lead her in a specific direction into which she may not wish to go - or to get her to express opinions she genuinely does not support
- Ends up with the professional supplying the answer himself

For example:

'What do you see as the issues which will impact upon your business plans in the future?... For instance how do you see the impending EC green legislation affecting the way you do business?... Do you think that this is going to make life more difficult for you and raise your costs?... I guess it has to doesn't it?'

What was intended as a good information-seeking question ends up as a rhetorical question. The prospective client really does not need to be consulted. A nod of the head will suffice if a question is posed in this way - hardly conducive to the open dialogue and rapport we are seeking to build in an early meeting with a prospect.

Multiple choice questions

The last example is also an example of what is called the multiple choice question. We have asked people who have a tendency to ask a lot of these types of questions why this is so. They give a number of reasons including:

- They are not sure that they have made the question very clear

- They think of a better (sometimes unconnected!) question as they are putting their first attempt into words

- They believe that the client does not understand the question

- When the client pauses for thinking time the questioner 'loses his nerve' in the short silence and continues by embellishing the question

- In their heart of hearts they want the client to agree with them so they give enough clues in the questions as to what is the 'correct' answer

Whatever the reason for the multiple choice question it is a demonstration of poor information-seeking. Imagine a prospective client on the end of this multiple choice effort:

> 'So where do you see your company in five years' time? I mean what are your objectives as an organisation?... Will you have to expand into the new market areas or will you seek to focus in particular niches where you have relatively greater strength? For instance, what about your field service commitment - will you continue to develop this when products are ever more disposable?... Do you have plans yourselves to produce a long-life disposable range?'

When finally given the chance, where does the prospective client start? There are some interesting questions wrapped up (and lost) in this illustration. In all good faith the client may start with the last part of the question - talking about the merits and demerits of long-life disposable products. From our observations the rest of the questions are probably lost for ever.

The worst case scenario is when the professional, upon reviewing the meeting, states something to the effect of:

> 'I asked her about her company's future objectives and she never gave me an answer.'

CHOOSING QUESTIONS FOR AN EFFECTIVE FUNNEL PROCESS

The 'Opportunity/Project' funnels

Once there has been an in-depth discussion drawn out from following the 'Business' funnels, it is appropriate and logical to move the discussion closer to the specific area in which the professional has particular expertise. The final question under the heading 'Some examples of funnel opening questions which could be asked' (page 64) begins to move in this direction. The exploration of the business issues may in itself begin to surface opportunities and problems in which the professional has expertise.

Before we begin to state how we could be of assistance to the client we must firstly establish how close a match there is between what appears to be the client's requirements and what the professional's organisation can deliver. Again we cannot predict every question we may need to ask to establish the match between the client's requirements and the professional's capabilities. We can again however determine the funnel openers - those open general questions which get us into the key areas which need exploration.

There is a simple tool which we use for this. It is called the Offer Analysis. An Offer Analysis can have a number of dimensions. For the purpose of determining what questions we need to use as funnel openers we will keep this tool to its most basic two-dimensional format.

We take a piece of A4 paper and divide it down the middle. On the left hand side of the sheet we list all of the features of the product, service or capability which the firm could offer to a prospective client.

The definition of a feature is: Any fact about our potential offering to a client.

On the right hand side of the sheet of paper we list all of the funnel openers which will help us explore what relevance the feature has to the particular prospective client to whom we are speaking.

We have worked with numerous clients constructing Offer Analyses. No matter how detailed and apparently complex the product or capability, we have found that it is unusual to need more than nine funnel opening questions. Remember, this does not mean that we will only ask nine questions or fewer. What it means is that there are nine or fewer subject areas which we need to explore to determine the fit between what we can do and what the client requires. In each area we have the funnel opener formulated.

On the next page we have an example of an Offer Analysis formulated for a fictitious IT consultancy. The features are not listed in any particular order. The questions are listed in a potential 'batting order'. We stress the word 'potential' because when one asks an open general question the ensuing funnelling process can take us down any number of unpredictable avenues.

The answer to the question, 'What will your future IT platform look like?' may very quickly and logically cause the client to talk about future projects. Clearly this makes the funnel opener, 'What projects are planned for the future?' completely redundant.

The third column on this example indicates the features which could be assessed by exploring in depth the funnel opened by the question listed in column two.

There are three separate questions which could ascertain the value of this consultancy's geographical location to a potential client. However, if we find out that a prospective client only has offices in one city and has no intention of establishing any of its future IT infrastructure outside of this one location, then this is a feature which delivers no benefit - to this particular prospect.

Professionals unskilled in the selling process tend to stress the points about their firm which they see as being strengths or unique points. Unless these features deliver a potential benefit to the client, talking about them is a waste of breath. Emphasis on such points usually has the opposite effect to the one intended. In the scenario of the client only having one location, what could be the reaction of the prospective client who is listening to the consultant talk about his company's expanding geographical empire? Probably she is thinking something along the lines of:

> 'All these offices are of no consequence to me and they must cost a lot of money to run. I think if we need some help with the next IT project we should use someone who is local.'

Exploring the areas opened up by the Offer Analysis funnel openers enables us to focus our offer on those features in which the client will see value.

Table 4.1: Offer Analysis for IT Consultancy Services Limited

	Features	Questions	Features explored
1	130 full-time consultants	What is your current and future IT platform?	5,6,7
2	Access to 250 specialist associates		
3	Ten offices around the UK	Where is it today and where will it be located in the future?	3,4
4	Offices in Paris, Bonn, Brussels		
5	Project experience of all major hardware vendors	What projects are planned for the future?	3,4,5,6,7, 9,12
6	Project experience of all major integrated software packages		
7	Data and Tele Comms expertise/ capability	How will/should these projects be approached and managed?	13,14,15, 16
8	Wide industry sector experience		
9	Capability to produce bespoke software	What internal capability/ capacity do you possess?	1,2,3,4,10, 11,13,14
10	Consultants with IT backgrounds		
11	Consultants with: - Financial - Manufacturing - Logistics backgrounds/experience	Who will be affected by future IT projects and developments?	16
12	'Runaway systems' expertise	What timescales will the projects have to meet?	1,2,13,15
13	Proven Project Management methodology and tools		
14	Proven methodology and tools for software selection and implementation	What do you seek from an outside source of assistance?	1 to 15
15	Proven concurrent engineering tools/processes		
16	Experience of managing change caused by IT developments		

THE MEETING SO FAR

Let us now summarise the points covered so far and put them in the context of the whole meeting. We have gone through the following stages:

1. We have positioned ourselves and our organisation at the beginning of the meeting. We have outlined what we see as the aims and format of the meeting and have ascertained if the client has any additional agenda points.

2. We have explained to the prospective client the reasons for our searching questions and the value to her of answering these questions.

3. We have developed an understanding of the prospective client's business and the issues it faces by exploring the 'Business' funnels.

4. We have moved on to explore any potential fit between what the prospective client may require and our organisation's capabilities by exploring the funnels suggested by creating an Offer Analysis.

We are forming a framework for the initial meeting - not a rigid straitjacket. The questions described above must not become a 'questionnaire' which the professional uses to interrogate the prospective client. They become an aide mémoire which the professional has to hand, to use as necessary. Preparing in this way helps to ensure that:

•   The 'best' questions are asked, not just the best ones that come to mind at the time.

•   The professional gathers as comprehensive a level of information as time allows - no key areas are missed.

•   The professional does not need to use precious mental energy in thinking of the next funnel opener. He can relax and focus all of his attention on listening to and understanding the prospective client's replies and on 'funnelling' these replies skilfully.

To work well within this framework the professional needs to be very flexible - particularly in responding to the answers which emanate from the initial funnel opening questions. He must be able to adapt to the information he receives. He must be capable of picking up the signals - both spoken and unspoken. He must be capable of summarising his understanding of the client's position at the drop of a hat and should be able to reflect accurately the client's feelings.

As in developing any skill, the professional needs to study and understand what best practice looks like. From there the next step is to practise.

Figure 4.3: Planning the subjects to explore

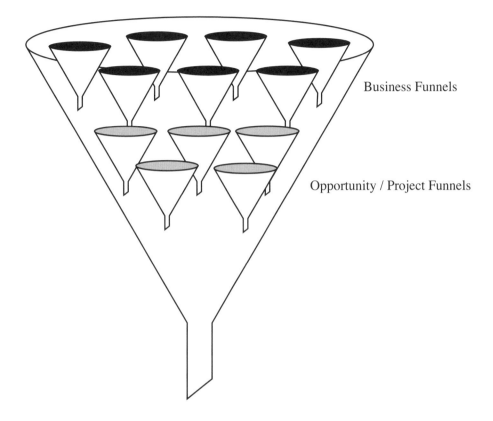

Business Funnels

Opportunity / Project Funnels

CHOOSING QUESTIONS FOR AN EFFECTIVE FUNNEL PROCESS

The 'Commercial' funnels

If ever there was a set of questions which professionals fail to ask or tend to avoid asking, it is the 'Commercial' funnel openers. How do we know this? On hundreds of seminars professionals tell us this is so. These same people also give us anecdote after anecdote relating to the problems and failures they have been involved in by failing to explore these issues.

There are five commercial areas to explore. They are:

1. The Basis of Decision (BOD).

2. The money or budgetary issues.

3. The competitive situation.

4. The timescales.

5. The Decision-Making Process (DMP).

Why do people avoid these issues? The most common reason we have been given is that people feel awkward in raising these questions. There is a fear that raising these questions could be seen as being 'unprofessional'.

We would see other behaviours as much more unprofessional. Producing a proposal which is costed at ten times the prospective client's expectations is highly unprofessional. Wasting a week producing a proposal which has no earthly chance of being successful we also believe is unprofessional. Responding to the prospective client so quickly that the client uses the proposal as a basis of discussion with other providers again is unprofessional. All of these scenarios are easily avoided if the 'Commercial' funnels are explored.

The word 'professional' quite clearly has different connotations - depending on one's viewpoint. If one is speaking with a prospective client with a highly tuned commercial culture, the senior management may look upon a professional who fails to explore the 'Commercial' funnels as extremely unprofessional!

The professional who is good at exploring the 'Commercial' issues is in a good position to formulate a plan or strategy to win the client. In Chapter Six, 'Strategies That Win New Clients', the value of this line of questioning will become even more evident.

What can be unprofessional is asking these questions in such a way that the client is made to feel uncomfortable or guarded in her response. In this section we will look not only at the questions but also how they may be phrased.

1. The Basis of Decision (BOD)

Professional   It is quite clear to me that your company is very firm in its decision to review the whole aspect of Duty and how you can minimise its effect on your business. As you said yourself, this is something you have neither the time nor expertise to tackle with internal resources. Can I ask you, in coming to a decision as to who you will use, what will be the most important factors the organisation will consider?

What the professional is aiming to do with this question is to open up, explicitly, the Basis of Decision (BOD) issue. Too often professionals guess at what is important to the client when she is making her decision. They try to read into the gist of the conversation what is important. Sometimes they are right and sometimes they are wrong. The professional who has explored the BOD funnel knows.

At times the prospective client can come back with a generic non-answer. We have to be ready for these.

Client   We want someone who is responsive, offers us good service, has people we can work with and of course is competitive fee-wise.

This is a classic non-answer. At this stage the professional has to put his listening and questioning skills to use and unbundle this. This is the skill we referred to earlier in this chapter in the section entitled 'Demonstrating our Listening'.

Professional   I'm anxious that we can demonstrate all of these attributes to you. When you say 'responsive', what exactly are you looking for and how would you like us to be able to demonstrate this to you?

This is the beginning of another funnel. Funnels exploring 'good service' and 'people we can work with' will also need to be opened, not to mention the question of 'competitive fee-wise'.

The BOD question can be explored in other dimensions. The question at the beginning of this section was phrased in such a way as to explore the organisation's Basis of Decision. This may be subtly different from the individual's Basis of Decision. The experienced professional, knowing that decisions are made and influenced by people, not organisations, will also explore this angle.

At the end of the funnels to unbundle what has previously been said, the professional may also ask:

Professional   Thank you for that. What about you? Are there any particular aspects that you personally will be looking for, from the people who help you with this?

Who knows what might come back? It could be:

Client   I'd like someone who will keep me advised of recommendations as they are forming. I personally need to be ahead of the game here. If the final conclusions are issued to all at the same time, there may be the odd person who will want to use the conclusions to their own end. I don't want to manipulate the conclusions, I just want to be sure that no one else is able to try that. I trust this is strictly off the record?

Valuable. One big step up for the professional who knows. A big disadvantage to the competing professional who does not know.

Professional   You also mentioned that your Chairman has been involved in the thinking behind this project. What things do you believe he will be looking for from the people who are selected to work on this?

Another dimension to the BOD question.

2. The monetary or budgetary issues

(Un)professional   How big is your budget?

Professionals tell us all the time that this is the question they really find difficult to ask. At the same time they also tell us stories of clients whose faces showed horror when they reached the page of the proposal on which the fees were outlined. They tell us of £35,000 proposals where the client had an expectation of 'two, maybe three thousand pounds'. They tell us of proposals where every effort was made to produce a lean and mean solution with fees to match - only to find out later that a competitor offering a much bigger and more expensive solution won easily.

We won't always get the information but the only 'crime' is not to try.

Professional   We could approach this project in a number of ways. For instance . . . . One key factor which will determine the way we formulate the final proposal will be determined by the budget you have allocated to this project. Could you give me an indication of the figure(s) you had in mind?

In this example the professional has opened up the subject by giving a good reason why the information may be valuable to the prospective client. Different ways of approaching solutions clearly have different cost implications.

Another way of introducing the subject could be:

Professional   With projects like this, when clients require outside assistance we find
                  that some clients have a fixed and determined budget for the work whilst
                  at the other end of the spectrum some clients find the money as and
                  when. How does it work in your organisation?

Some prospective clients do not have allocated budgets for professional advice. Asking
them directly about their budget could be a source of embarrassment and a very good
reason why we sometimes get answers like, 'That's for me to know and you to find out.'

A way of raising the subject that some of us use is to smile broadly and say:

Professional   I know you'd think me unprofessional if I didn't ask - so I will. What
                  sort of investment do you have in mind for this work?

It is the broad smile that makes the question acceptable.

It must be remembered that these examples are just funnel openers. The professional must
listen to the answers and question further.

Other subsidiary questions which may occur further down the funnel are:

- What does the budget include and exclude?

- What other budgets could be utilised?

- How flexible is the budget?

- Who is the budget-holder?

- What are the sign-off thresholds?

- When does the budgetary period begin and end?

- What would happen if some more monies had to be found?

The professional in possession of this information is far better placed than his polite
counterpart who thought these subjects too sensitive to raise.

3. The competitive situation

Professional   You're talking with us today about this - it's an opportunity which we
                  appreciate. Can I ask: what other alternatives are you considering in
                  order to resolve this issue?

Al Ries and Jack Trout, the authors of such authoritative works as Marketing Warfare and
Positioning, argue that the most important issue in the sales and marketing mix is your
position in relation to your competitors. Of the three 'C' elements, namely Customers,
Corporation and Competitors, they state that the most important of these is your
competitors - more important even than your customers.

We don't want to enter that debate here, but most times we will not be working in a
vacuum. There will be other competitors and alternative solutions to ours. We have to
position our final proposal to be better than the others. If we do not know what those other
alternatives are, then how do we best position ourselves?

Note the question the professional has posed. He has not asked, 'Who are our competitors?'. He has asked about the 'other alternatives' which may be considered.

The prospective client may reply:

Client   Well, as you'd expect, we are talking to a couple of other people like yourselves, but there is also a possibility that we may use some internal people for this. It's another option.

The professional needs to open up the funnels indicated by the prospect with questions such as:

Professional   What would cause you to decide to use your own resources?

Professional   You said that you would be talking with others. This makes eminent sense. May I be so bold as to ask who else you will be talking to?

We will not always get the response we want to this question. Clients have said to us in the past, 'I won't tell you who they are and I won't tell them that I am talking to you.' However, far more people have told us, 'I don't mind you knowing at all. We've already seen... and we plan to talk to... '

Knowing who we are up against helps us in the way we will formulate our arguments and ultimate proposal. We will definitely put a different slant on our proposal if we are competing against a niche player compared to a mainstream competitor. Sometimes asking the 'alternatives' question can give us insight into how serious the prospective client is about seeking help. Someone who is talking to a dozen different providers may well be trawling the market for free information. In this case an early response via a proposal would be wholly inappropriate.

We have heard the argument:

> 'If I ask the client who they are also talking with, it may put the idea in their minds that they should be talking to other providers. They might not have thought of that.'

This is the ultimate insult to a client's intelligence. Clients buy products and services on a daily basis. Their businesses survive on the difference between the selling price of their products and services and the costs they have to meet. If a client is going to talk to three alternative providers she will already have thought of this. On the other hand if the client is convinced she wants to talk only with the people she believes to be best placed to carry out the work, she will pursue this course of action.

There is no danger in asking the 'alternatives' question. The only danger lies in ignorance.

4. The timescales

This is a fundamental funnel to explore if we are to formulate a meaningful strategy to win the prospective client's work. The following is an oft-repeated scene from the offices of one of our previous employers.

The time is 4.30 p.m. and a rather new, inexperienced consultant rushes into the building. He drops his briefcase by his desk and approaches his secretary - a very experienced lady with an in-depth understanding of the business. He has a wad of paper in his hand.

Consultant	Can you work late tonight?
Secretary	Why?
Consultant	I promised the prospect I saw this morning that we'd have this proposal on his desk by tomorrow.
Secretary	Oh? When will he make the decision?
Consultant	Look. I've promised him it will be there.
Secretary	So when will he make the decision?
Consultant	We have to be able to show that we are responsive. A proposal on his desk tomorrow will create the right impression.
Secretary	OK. Perhaps. So when is he going to make the decision?

At some point the penny drops. With some consultants who believed that no secretary could ever know more than they, the penny only dropped when they realised that they had a large number of proposals sitting on prospective clients' desks and these clients were strangely unavailable to take a telephone call.

We find that the rush to go into writing is often generated by the professional rather than the prospective client. The rather flawed thinking behind this goes somewhat as follows:

> Before a client makes a decision she must have something in writing - outlining exactly what she will get and what she will be paying. (Fair assumption.) Therefore the quicker I can get something in writing to the client, the quicker she can make the decision. (How naive!)

The professional who falls into this trap is concerned only with his selling process. He is totally unaware of the prospective client's buying process. He may be unaware that the prospect has not even engaged in a buying process.

A colleague from the past used to illustrate this phenomenon in the following words:

> 'And the creaking noise that emanated from the North that evening was another Scandinavian forest being felled to produce proposals written on the back of one-hour meetings.'

The premature proposal is a Godsend to competitors. On the assumption that a buying decision will be reached, the experienced professional, knowing the timescales, will be using this time to further his case. He will also be using the time to alter the frames of reference for the work - to his own advantage.

'Mr Efficient' who sent his proposal in the day after the meeting has a submission which is gathering dust as it is being made redundant. This is a subject we will return to in Chapter Six, 'Strategies That Win New Clients'.

There are three dimensions to the timescales funnel and we would suggest that in most cases they should be addressed in the following order.

- When do you want the outputs from this project to be producing results for you?

- When do you therefore envisage that the project should begin?

- When therefore have you decided to reach a decision as to which route you will pursue for this project?

Professionals tell us constantly of clients who take ages to make up their minds and then expect that the work can start tomorrow and produce results the day after. They also tell us that they did not bring up the 'timescales' questions.

Many times clients have not thought through the time question in any detail. By asking the three questions above in the suggested order one can sometimes enable the client to realise she has an imminent decision to make.

5. The Decision-Making Process (DMP)

The scene is a workshop, the subject is the Decision-Making Process.

Participant	People lie about this.
Facilitator	Sorry?
Participant	They never tell you the truth when you ask them.
Facilitator	What exactly are you asking them?
Participant	About who makes the final decision of course. People always lie. They always say, 'It's me.' You find out later they were lying but it's too late by then. It's not worth asking the question. I don't bother now.

The participant is right. It is definitely not worth asking that question - particularly in that way.

Facilitator	Why do you want to know who makes the final decision?
Participant	(Beginning to question the facilitator's 'street cred'.) That's obvious That's who you need to be selling to.

The proposition was that we should sell to the MAN - the person with the Money, Authority and Need. This line of thinking originates from early writing on sales technique. There is an assumption that this is one and the same person - very often incorrect. There is a further assumption that the MAN will be accessible during the selling process. The real world is not always so kind to us.

What we need to find out is the process which the organisation will go through before a decision is reached.

We may phrase the question something like:

Professional	You've told me that you need to make a decision before the end of next month if this is going to meet the implementation dates you have in mind. Can I ask you: what will be the processes which will happen within the organisation between today and the 30th April in order that the decision is finally reached?

This is the beginning of what may be a quite extensive funnel. Sub-questions which may suggest themselves could be:

• Who will become involved in this process?

• At what stage will they become involved?

- What will their function be in the process?

- What will their Bases of Decision be?

We have found that by trying to understand the full Decision-Making Process, it often becomes evident who makes the final decision. Whether and how they can be reached is another question.

By following the full Decision-Making Process (DMP) funnel we begin to understand the organisation to whom we are selling. By defining the process we can begin to consider our appropriate approach and strategy. Many clients will not have thought through what the process will be. This should not be unexpected. This is not like placing an order for business stationery. Most clients do not decide to employ professional advisers on a daily basis. The last time they went about it may have no relevance to how they will do it this time.

The professional who enters the DMP funnel with the 'unprepared' client can discover with this client what needs to happen in order to select an appropriate provider. The professional who fails to raise the question trusts to luck and hopes for competitors as 'gentlemanly' as he.

CHOOSING QUESTIONS FOR AN EFFECTIVE FUNNEL PROCESS

The 'Sweep-up' question

The 'Sweep-up' is used at the end of each funnel and when we believe we have explored every funnel. It is usually phrased as a closed question. There are many ways of expressing the question. One way could be:

Professional   1. At the end of one funnel: "I believe I now have a good understanding of how you see the market developing over the next five years. Just before I check my understanding is accurate is there anything else you think I should know about future developments in the marketplace?"

2. When we believe we have explored every funnel: "You have given me a good overall picture of the organisation and the potential significance of the Duty issue on your future decisions. We've also explored in some depth the type of assistance you require and what will be important to you. Is there anything else which you think it would be helpful for me to know?

Figure 4.4: Planning the subjects to explore

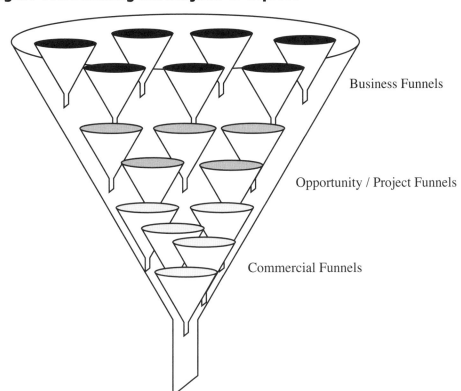

Business Funnels

Opportunity / Project Funnels

Commercial Funnels

The question may or may not bring new information. The professional should be pleased if nothing more emerges. This demonstrates the thoroughness with which he has conducted what has gone before.

There is no risk in asking the 'Sweep-up' question - only potential gains. The only risk is in not asking. The question should therefore be asked in every information gathering meeting. If there is more information, the client's response should be funnelled. Continue asking the question, perhaps phrased differently until the client says, 'No, I think that's everything.'

However, we have also seen and heard professionals use the 'Sweep-up' too early in a meeting, as soon as they have surfaced what they believe is one potential issue with a client.

Professional   That's interesting. Apart from that, is there anything else?

This repetitive and obvious technique is used for the rest of the meeting. This may suffice in a role-play in which the client is generous and 'nice'. It will not pass muster in a real meeting.

MOVING FROM THE AC TO THE ES OF THE PACES PROCESS

This is the time for a major summary. The professional will be in possession of a lot of well-won information at this point. Now the most salient points have to be brought together to form a well-rounded picture of the issues, problems or opportunities which the prospective client faces. The summary is not a boring repetition of what the client has just said. It should encapsulate the key issues in an accurate and interesting 'picture of the situation as I see it, Ms Client'.

One of the benefits of doing this is that sometimes in the course of summarising in this way, the professional can pull together what may have previously been seen by the client as disparate issues - and make connections between them. The professional can bring clarity. The professional may also bring new insight to the client. The client may begin to see the picture in a new way. This is a demonstration of expertise - helping to build an image of competence in the client's eye.

At the end of this summary it is worth asking the 'Sweep-up' one more time in case anything has been missed. In any initial meeting the aim is to progress as far through this process as possible.

When we have asked professionals how long prospective clients normally put aside for an initial exploratory meeting the answer we most often receive is, '45 minutes to an hour'. There are exceptions. If one comes highly recommended to the prospective client it is less of a risk to the prospect to give an hour and a half or even two hours.

Working on the assumption that we have checked with the prospect and we have an hour for the meeting, we need to leave ourselves ten to fifteen minutes to:

> **E** xplore or explain a suitable way forward.

> **S** eek commitment to the suggested way forward.

This means that the questioning and active listening phase of the meeting has to be completed in 35 to 40 minutes - assuming five minutes or a little more to get the meeting under way.

How can we ensure that we reach a point where, after 40 minutes, we have something to work on, something to explore further with the client, something which the client sees as an issue important enough to dedicate further time to?

Firstly, follow the structure. It works. Secondly, practise. The professional who practises more often will develop a better feel for when he needs to pursue a funnel further. He will realise more quickly when he is obtaining information for the sake of collecting information. He will learn to summarise quickly and move the discussion forward.

There are times when it is impossible to explore all of the 'Business', 'Offer Analysis' and 'Commercial' funnels in one meeting. In this case the professional will know exactly what has been explored and what remains to be examined.

Chapter 5 PACES:
Gaining Commitment

INTRODUCTION

Closing the sale

Over the years we have had many requests to 'train my people how to close the sale. They're good with their clients but they just don't seem to be able to ask the killing question.' This request invariably comes from an individual who either does not understand the selling and buying processes or has never taken the time to observe what really happens when his people are in front of clients and prospective clients - or both!

Most selling is not about slick 'tricks' or 'closing techniques' which somehow get the client to say 'Yes' (against her better judgement). Selling professional services to prospective clients is particularly unsuited to any practices which have any taint of trickery about them. In most instances when a client decides to use a professional for the first time, the client is intensely aware that this is a potential on-going relationship which is being entered into. The client knows that she will have to work with these people - and perhaps have to work closely with them.

To compare this to a potential marriage may be overstating the situation to some extent. However, the analogy is not wholly inappropriate. Marriage normally occurs after a period of courtship - a period of 'getting to know you'. The prospective client is not being coy with the intent of wanting to appear virtuous or hard to get. The prospect genuinely needs to make the right choice. The wrong choice has potentially disastrous implications.

Focusing on the right process

Many professionals we work with for the first time want hints and tips which will enable them to win new clients more quickly. They want to run a more effective selling process. This focus is understandable. It is also mostly wrong. Such a focus is more likely to turn prospective clients away because the behaviours which indicate this hurried way of thinking will make themselves manifest to the prospect. To quote Maister again: 'My impressions and perceptions are created by small actions that are meaningful for their symbolism...'

Radical as the advice may seem initially, we recommend that professionals should forget about their focus on their selling process. Instead they should try to ascertain and understand the prospective client's likely buying process - and use this as the basic framework for developing the relationship.

If we pause for a minute let us consider a business that typically takes six months to a year to make a significant commitment to a new supplier. Why should Tricky John who has just been on the latest course on closing the sale succeed in one meeting? Is there likely to be such a magic formula which has somehow eluded us for the whole of our professional lives?

The professional needs to understand from an early stage the processes which the prospective client is likely to go through when appointing a new provider.

This is one purpose of opening the 'Commercial' funnels related to the Decision-Making Process, the Basis of Decision and the timescales involved.

Even when our first meeting puts us in front of a decisive individual, this person alone may not make the decision for the organisation. There will usually be other decision influencers up and down the organisation who will need to be involved.

It could be argued that if we are dealing with the MAN (the person with the Money, Need and Authority - and the will to appoint us) why would we want to get involved with other people who only have influence? After all, some of that influence could be negative to our approach.

The answer is simple. If there are people who could be negative to our appointment, it is usually better to meet with them before the appointment is made. If they are presented with a fait accompli and feel they have not been consulted on a subject on which they have meaningful input, they may become sleeping insurrectionists - people who stealthily sabotage the work we carry out in the assignment.

The right level of commitment

All of the above does not mean that we should do our best and just wait for the client to decide when the time is right. We should maintain the initiative and work towards the highest possible level of client commitment at each stage. As the process progresses we can build that commitment at the right speed for the client - no faster and no slower.

The conclusion is that we must seek a commitment at the end of our initial meeting which the prospective client will be comfortable with. From our perspective, we must seek real commitment from the prospect. At first glance these two objectives may seem to conflict. They don't.

If, for instance, the professional seeks the following commitment at the end of the meeting there may be a problem:

Professional   Well, from our discussion you have an on-going need for legal
                      representation on litigation issues. This product liability suit, whilst

obviously a big concern for yourselves, provides us with an ideal opportunity. I would propose that you appoint us to represent you on this case. As I have outlined over the last few minutes, we have the experience and expertise to handle this. This really is our cup of tea. Could we handle this case for you?

On the assumption that the prospective client already has a firm (or a number of firms) in which it has faith to carry out the discussed case, the new provider is asking for too much. An hour after walking in off the street the eager professional is certainly asking for a commitment - but the feeling of the prospective client will be one of uncertainty and probably discomfort.

A very typical client response to such a 'close', could be:

Client   Well we intend to talk to a couple of people whom we have worked with in the past on cases like this. I tell you what, why don't you send me a proposal?

We're back to the possibility of Scandinavian forests being felled again.

The professional who responds in the affirmative to this request is in the situation of carrying through a next stage with which the prospective client is comfortable - but which demonstrates no commitment from the client.

So what is commitment? The 'golden rule' on commitment is that:

Commitment involves the prospective client in action.

In other words commitment is about getting the prospect to become involved in a buying process - but involved at a level and a pace with which they are comfortable.

Explain or Explore a way forward

Toward the end of the questioning phase and at the point where the professional is summarising the whole picture, the brain really has to go into overdrive. At this stage the professional also needs to be concluding what commitment he will try to seek from the prospect and what he will need to say to convince the prospect to give this commitment. Not surprisingly, we have observed that listening skills are usually at their nadir at this point in the meeting. The brain cannot cope very well with the conflicting demands being made upon it.

One question which needs to be answered concerns how we position the way forward. Do we follow the advice of some and offer the prospective client a choice of ways forward (the exploration method) or do we simply give what we believe is the best way ahead (the explain approach)? There are advocates for both approaches. The supporters of the first approach are firmly convinced that most people prefer to have considered a number of options before they make up their minds with regard to any significant decision. The proponents of the second approach argue that if the professional is the expert on the subject and has previous experience then he, as the specialist, should advise the client as to the best next step. Choices would only serve to offer second-best alternatives.

The correct answer to the question is that both camps are right - depending on the circumstances. The only wrong answer comes from the person who takes a dogmatic view and insists that he follows the one route every time.

This is where the professional has to demonstrate flexibility. The best road forward will be determined by two main factors:

1.   The professional's previous track record of the problem, opportunity or issue faced by the prospect.

The more experience the professional has, the more likely he will be able to give advice as to the best next step. If a professional has extensive experience he is also more likely to sound convincing as he outlines the best way forward.

2.   The likely response of the client to being offered alternatives or just 'one best way' forward.

If during the meeting the prospective client utters words like 'We're looking for someone to tell us what to do', this is a different message from 'I'm looking at this problem and trying to find alternative ways we can deal with it.'

In the first example the prospect is unlikely to warm to the professional who gives four choices. She wants to know the best suggestion from the expert. Equally, an approach aimed at convincing the client there is only one suitable way ahead will not be well received in the second example.

So, having summarised the prospect's overall position, how could the meeting go from there?

Example

Professional	Does that about encapsulate the issue you face and position it correctly?
Client	Yes, I think you have a good understanding.
Professional	OK, Jill, I know we can help you here and we would be very interested to do so. What I would like to do for a few minutes is to tell you about how we have helped other clients in a similar position and the benefits we have brought to them. Then I'd like to explore a couple of different ways that we can take this forward and agree with you the next step you'd like us to take. Is that OK?
Client	Sure. I'm waiting to hear what you think.

The professional is positive and assertive. '... I know we can help you here...'

He tells the prospective client he wants their business.'... we would be very interested...'

This is not the time to be hesitant and uncertain. People are not likely to take advice from those who are unsure. However, he has picked up the signs that this client does not want to be presented with one solution. He knows that offering alternatives does not have to be a sign of uncertainty. This is conveyed in the manner of the delivery of the message.

He is also sensitive to the fact that any next step has to be a joint agreement. A successful conclusion to the meeting cannot be the imposition of one party's preferred way forward.

Professional	As I said, the situation you have described has a number of elements which are common to other successful projects we've been involved in. How we've been able to help clients in the past is by...

At this point the professional has to give enough information to establish that he and his organisation have the expertise and track record to be considered potential candidates for the work which needs to be done. Expertise and track record are two elements of demonstrating competence - one of the essentials for beginning to build trust.

After a few minutes of demonstrating competence in this way, we pick up the meeting again.

Professional	...In summary I am certain we could do this work for you. Let me give you a couple of ways in which we could take this forward.

One alternative we could follow would be for me to meet with all of the people who have a major input into this issue. The purpose of these meetings would be twofold. Firstly I would seek their views and their concerns; and secondly, on the basis of their inputs I would put together a short presentation. I would then deliver this to all concerned - probably within a week of my final meeting. This presentation would be aimed at presenting you with a short list of the potential methods the business could adopt in dealing with the problem - and giving their likely impact in respect of your particular organisation.

The benefit of this approach is that it will get you to the point of having all of your people involved and consulted and all knowing the possible avenues which exist in order to resolve the issue.

To do this I will need you to set up meetings with a number of the people you have mentioned during the meeting. I will need to spend time with the financial director and the financial controller. In addition your head of purchasing and your marketing director should also be included as they have an interest at either end of the chain. You may suggest one or two others but I believe these four are essential. In order that the presentation fits with all concerned, we will also need to agree a date for this.

If you're able to put these meetings in place then I am very happy to make the necessary investment of my time.

Alternatively, we are running a half-day workshop on this very subject in a month's time. At this seminar we introduce specific case studies of clients for whom we have worked - helping them to resolve the kind of problems you're facing.

It's rather easy for me to tell you in a space of five minutes that we are well equipped to handle this sort of thing but perhaps you would like to hear more of how we go about it and have the opportunity of speaking with some of our existing clients. I would be very happy for you to attend as my guest on the day and to meet with you shortly after the workshop to discuss your situation again - once you have a closer feel of how we tackle this type of assignment.

Some people we have worked with would take issue with the two alternatives suggested above. Their bone of contention goes something like this:

> "Well all this person is doing is giving things away. In one instance he's giving away his professional time and in the second he is giving away a free place on a seminar. Anyone can give stuff away. We've got to be able to sell these things. They have value and the client should pay".

A very macho approach... and also a very unsuccessful one.

David Maister, in his article, 'How Clients Choose' has some words on this topic:

> "Maybe I'll agree to meet one of your specialist partners, or consent to provide additional information to you, or provide access to one of my other executives. Perhaps I'll participate in one of your seminars or agree an additional, more focused meeting. Any one of these things should be taken as a success. If you try to rush me, I'll take it as a sign that you're more interested in making a sale than helping me".

In the example we have used, the professional has asked for specific commitments in both alternatives.

In the first case he has asked for the time of a number of senior executives - firstly in a one-on-one situation and then all together. Perhaps more significantly he has asked his client contact to 'risk' her credibility by putting him in front of some significant players from within the business. He has asked for a lot.

In the second case he has asked a senior person within the business to give up a half a day of her time to learn more about his firm. Yes, she should benefit from the experience - but she will have to give up the time. The professional has already stated that a follow-up meeting is a further commitment he will also be seeking.

Potential ways forward

There are many ways in which the professional could seek to take the dialogue further forward. Some of these options include:

- Agreement to a meeting or presentation at our offices
- Agreement that the prospective client will prepare and send a specification for the task/project discussed
- Agreement to a further meeting - with the prospective client responsible for inviting other interested parties
- Agreement that the person we have met will effect an introduction to a more relevant contact within the organisation
- Agreement that the prospect will arrange a series of one-to-one meetings in order that the project can be better understood and scoped
- Agreement to our returning to present a discussion document to all concerned

Seek commitment to the suggested way forward

This must be the most over-hyped subject in selling. In the Tricky John sales training course one learns 25 (or some equally ridiculous number of) ways to close the sale and get the unwilling client to say, 'Yes'. This is bunkum.

In our scenario the prospective client has now spent 55 minutes of a one-hour meeting weighing up this professional seated across from her. Take it as read - she will already have decided if she wants the dialogue to go further. She will already have come to her conclusions in respect of credibility, competence and compatibility. No trick in the last five minutes is going to change anything at all. In fact any attempt will simply backfire and damage the professional's credibility.

Avoid the temptations to try the seemingly plausible techniques such as the 'Half Nelson' which goes something like this:

Client   What you've told me is interesting and something we may have to examine further. Do you ever carry out this work in out-of-hours situations - say after 5.00 p.m. or at weekends?

Professional   If we could do that would you agree to go ahead and give us the contract?

Yuk!!

If the professional has followed the PACES process then he will not have to be concerned with 'closing'. In this case:

• He will have prepared carefully and in detail

• He will have made a positive first impression

• He will have positioned himself and his organisation clearly and coherently

• He will have made it clear that he wants to understand the client's position

• He will have explored the client's situation and requirements in detail using thought-through questions

• He will have demonstrated real understanding through active listening

• He will have encapsulated the whole picture in one final summary

• He will have succinctly presented why his firm is capable of working with the prospective client

• He will have put forward one or two logical and convincing alternatives for the way ahead

The way ahead will be obvious to both parties. The client will usually volunteer the commitment. If, on the other hand, the PACES process has largely been ignored for a more 'free-flowing and adaptable' (read unplanned, unprepared, unstructured and unprofessional) approach, then no super close is going to make the slightest difference.

What about the meetings which fall somewhere in between? There may be times when it is not clear if we have the prospective client's commitment. Then we have to ask.

Forget the other 23 methods. There are two which are common sense, acceptable and professional. One is called the basic close. With the basic close the professional is simply asking the prospective client a straight question.

It may go something as follows:

Professional	...So, based on our experience, that would be the best way to deal with this, and the round table discussion with your technical people should be the next step. Can we organise this for some time in the next two weeks?

The question requires a simple answer. If it gets a 'Yes' then all is fine; if it gets a less than total acceptance then there is some resistance which needs to be understood and dealt with.

The other acceptable way of asking for commitment is the alternative close. This is suited to the situations where we may have put a couple of suggested ways forward to the prospective client.

For example:

Professional	...So we could go forward either way. We can go down the route of meeting with your people and then putting together a presentation or you can come along to our seminar and we can meet again after that.
	Which would you prefer?

Again the client is asked a simple question. This time she has two alternatives to choose from. Again, there could potentially be hesitation with both of these. The likelihood of this is in inverse proportion to the quality of the rest of the meeting which has preceded this point.

We have yet to meet the person who is genuinely competent in carrying through selling meetings with clients and prospective clients but whose sole shortcoming is that he can't close and ask for commitment. Our bet is that we will never meet that person.

Handling resistance

Professional	...So, in summary I believe that the way forward would be for you and your two co-directors to attend one of our half-day focus group workshops. This would not only give you some specific ideas as to how we can help but will also allow you to get a feel for our professionalism and the chemistry between our organisation and yours.
	Shall I reserve you a place on our workshop on the 12th or do you think it would be more suitable next month on the 15th?
Client	I'm not sure that that would be appropriate. It seems to me that we may be rushing things somewhat.
Professional	OK. If you want to do this later on, that is no problem. As I said earlier we run these focus group workshops on a regular basis - every month in fact with the exception of August and December. Perhaps you would like to attend one of our early Autumn workshops?
Client	Possibly ...I'll have to think about it.

Professional	Sure. Is there any other information I can give you before I leave?
Client	No, I don't think so. It's been an interesting meeting. Thanks for coming along.

Five minutes later the professional is sitting in his car. He is going back over the meeting in his mind. The opening was punchy and professional. He had spent time understanding the prospective client's situation and requirements. Some real needs which his firm could address had emerged. The client had acknowledged that these issues needed to be addressed and that they were willing to invest money in a solution. He had established that the t would be made by joint agreement between the three executive directors and they were not talking to anyone else right now. A couple of potential competitors had already been ruled out by the client. It had all looked so promising!

But it had all gone wrong at the end. He had suggested a logical first step, quite a small initial step, the sort of first step that most prospective clients would easily say 'Yes' to. He had sought commitment - and had received a rejection. He had tried hard to retrieve the situation but had left with the, 'I'll think about it' words ringing in his ear.

What had gone wrong?

On the basis that the professional's diagnosis that the P, A and C of the PACES process was right, the problems must have occurred somewhere in the E and S.

Let us look at an alternative way he may have managed the closing section of this meeting.

Professional	...So, in summary I believe that the way forward would be for you and your two co-directors to attend one of our half-day focus group workshops. This would not only give you some specific ideas as to how we can help but will also allow you to get a feel for our professionalism and the chemistry between our organisation and yours.
	Shall I reserve you a place on our workshop on the 12th or do you think it would be more suitable next month on the 15th?
Client	I'm not sure that that would be appropriate. It seems to me that we may be rushing things somewhat.
Professional	(Pauses - waiting for prospective client to continue and expand on what she has said.)
Client	I would need to discuss this with my co-directors.
Professional	What parts exactly would you need to discuss?
Client	Well it's the whole thing about the three of us coming along to one of these workshops.
Professional	Is there some specific problem with that idea?
Client	Well, George our Technical Director has a real concern with these types of events. It goes back to a similar thing he was invited to a couple of years ago. The discussions on the workshop were meant to be totally

confidential but he found out otherwise some time later. Beyond that I really don't want to go into the details of what happened but I know that he will not attend and I believe he will try to discourage John and me from participating.

Professional	Correct me if I'm wrong but during our meeting I picked up the feeling that you have an issue here which you are all anxious to resolve. I also felt that you were positive to the outline I gave of how we could help. However, the way ahead I have suggested seems inappropriate. Have I got that right?
Client	You're absolutely spot on. We do want to move forward on this but if attending a focus group workshop is the only way ahead we have a problem of acceptance.
Professional	OK, I'm sure we can sort out that problem, but let me ask: are there any other issues which would stop us taking a next step together - providing of course that the next step is acceptable to you and your co-directors?
Client	Only the chemistry thing.
Professional	(Pauses - waiting for prospective client to continue and expand on what she has said.)
	The chemistry thing?
Client	Yes. Whilst I take your idea of the workshop being a good opportunity to assess the chemistry between your organisation and ours, it is our belief that what is even more important is the chemistry between the professional who works with us and the key people in our organisation who will be involved.
	For instance, I believe that you would fit very well with the type of people we are. There may be other people in your organisation who would not. If we were to invest any further time with you we would want to be assured at this point that we would be working with individuals whom we felt comfortable with. There's no point in going any further now if we find out in three months time that your best qualified person for this type of work simply doesn't fit.
Professional	So you have a concern about who we may assign to this work and you want to be assured in some way that you would be working with individuals who are a good fit for you, your co-directors and members of your organisation with whom we may become involved?
Client	That's it.
Professional	Is there anything else that may stand in the way of us taking a next step together?
Client	No. I think I've thrown enough boulders in your path. I'm not trying to be difficult but you need to be aware of where we are coming from.

Professional	I understand completely - but if I can assure you on these two points I take it that you would be open to progressing beyond this meeting?
Client	Yes, of course.
Professional	All right, let me suggest another way forward which will address both of the points you have raised. I believe that getting you involved in a facilitated meeting format such as I originally suggested is the best way forward. However, we can vary the format of this. Instead of your attending one of our external focus-group workshops we can run one for a couple of hours here on your premises, exclusively for your company. To make it flow I would suggest involving some of your more senior managers as well as your co-directors.
	I have a person in mind who I believe will work extremely well in your business. He has the right background and credentials and he has the right way of thinking to work with your people. I would be happy to send you his CV but I think that in order to get the focus of our two-hour session totally right, it would be even more appropriate for Brian and me to come along and meet with you, your co-directors and the other people whom you think would give valuable input.
	Just short individual meetings would be fine - 20 to 30 minutes per person. These meetings will achieve two things. Firstly this investment of time from our side will help us in tailoring the workshop session. Secondly I know that from just a short meeting your people will be convinced that Brian has a lot to offer and they will welcome further contact with him.
	Now I understand your concerns I believe that this way ahead would be even better for you. What do you think?
Client	That's good. When would you and Brian want to come and meet us? I think it is more important to meet my co-directors and three of the senior managers than it is to spend a lot of time with me. You seem to have a good grasp of our situation and I have confidence that you wouldn't suggest this way forward unless you were convinced that it was going to work.
Professional	I think the sooner the better. I have a couple of alternatives the week after next but as soon as I get back to the office I'll check Brian's availability and get back to you this afternoon. How does that sound?
Client	Fine!

The immediately noticeable difference between these two scenarios is that the second one is far longer. This is because the professional has made every effort to understand the reasons for the prospective client's reluctance to proceed down a suggested path.

In the first scenario the professional attempts to formulate an alternative solution without knowing the problem he is trying to tackle. He immediately attempts to move into 'convince mode' when he should begin by engaging his 'listening mode'.

In the second example the professional is following a sound process. Once he hears that the client has some uncertainty about what he has suggested, he proceeds in the following way:

Step 1   Pause

Step 2   Question, listen and summarise (funnel) to understand the issue

Step 3   Ascertain if this is the only problem

Step 4   If there is another issue - question, listen and summarise (funnel)

Step 5   Check if there are any other issues

Step 6   Test. Is the client seeking solutions or will any suggestion be rejected?

Step 7   Provide solutions

Step 8   Seek commitment

Step 1: Pause

By pausing and not rushing in with either a solution or a question the professional potentially achieves four things:

1. The pause shows that he is thinking about what the client has said.

2. The pause does give genuine thinking time.

3. The pause may well encourage the prospective client to expand upon what she has said, for example: "What I mean is…", thus providing real insight into this issue.

4. If the client thinks as she talks, she may even create her own solution.

Step 2: Question, listen and summarise (funnel) to understand the issue

On the assumption that the client has not expanded upon her initial comment, or has not expanded fully, the professional then has to open up a funnel on the subject. An open general question such as, 'How do you mean?' may be appropriate to begin the exploration of the reason for resistance. As with any funnel the professional should summarise at the end to ensure that he has got a full and accurate understanding of the issue.

Step 3: Ascertain if this is the only problem

Having defined the reason for the resistance, the temptation is to jump in straight away and provide an answer - especially if the answer seems obvious. However, there is a danger that other problems still need to be surfaced.

In fact the first hurdle brought forward by the prospective client may not be the only one. There may be connections between the varying issues which the client raises. Therefore it is important to try to get them all out on the table.

Step 4: If there is another issue - question, listen and summarise (funnel)

This is a repeat of Step 2 should a further problem appear. Again the process should finish with a summary.

Step 5: Check if there are any other issues

This is a repeat of Step 3 - trying to dig out all of the potential issues.

Step 6: Test. Is the client seeking solutions or will any suggestion be rejected?

This is an optional step. If we are in any doubt about the real interest of the prospective client we may carry out the test step. We may also insert this step if our solutions to the issues raised are going to involve us in expending a lot of effort or time.

In the second scenario the professional chose to insert the test step with: 'I understand completely - but if I can assure you on these two points I take it that you would be open to progressing beyond this meeting?'

Step 7: Provide solutions

In the second scenario the professional was able to provide an alternative way forward on the spot. He was even able to link the two issues in one composite solution.

In some instances it may not be possible to provide an immediate answer. The prospective client may want a technical question answered. The answer may require research. An 'off-the-cuff' glib answer may be more of a credibility destroyer than the response, 'The last thing I want is to mislead you inadvertently. I don't have the answer. I'll have to check it out and get back to you.'

Step 8: Seek commitment

If we have provided convincing answers to the problems which the prospective client foresaw, then it is appropriate to ask for commitment.

If it is obvious that we want to understand the prospective client's concerns and we have then provided fitting solutions, commitment will often be volunteered. In the second example when the professional asked 'What do you think?' after he had suggested the alternative way forward, the client's response indicated that she was committed to the solution.

In the first scenario no amount of 'closing' would have succeeded. The professional did not understand the issues and was not able to put a viable solution forward.

MOVING BEYOND THE FIRST MEETING

Having now obtained commitment to a next step, the professional needs to map out a campaign to win the prospect and convert her organisation to client status. Some strategies are doomed to failure from the start. Others offer a far higher potential success rate.

In Chapter Six we examine the strategies that win new clients.

Section 4 **Strategies That Win New Clients**

Chapter 6 Strategies That Win New Clients

INTRODUCTION

We have met many professionals whose selling skills are adequate, and some whose skills are excellent, but who nevertheless achieve limited success. They tend to win small commissions from small prospects but have a poor track record in securing the big new clients which will significantly improve their business or help to make their name in the firm. These professionals often complain:

- 'It's not fair, I lost because of "politics"'

- 'They say they like our proposals but we always come second'

- 'The clients don't seem to recognise the best solutions when they see them - we had far more to offer than the firm they chose'

- 'She said she would have chosen us but her boss, who wasn't supposed to be involved, overrode her decision'

- 'They are happy with their existing advisers - how can we overcome that?'

It is our experience that a major cause of these frustrations lies in the professionals' natural inclination to act rather than think; to pursue the obvious path rather than to plan the approach which will win the client. Excellent selling skills are not enough to win major clients. These skills must be focused in the right way, on the right people and at the right time to secure a competitive advantage which will ensure the decision goes our way.

In this section we focus on how the professional should plan his, and his firm's, campaign toward each targeted prospect - how to move through the P3 section of the PACE Pipeline from a successful first meeting to create a significant new client. The ideas are not complicated.

They need to be simple if they are to work in a busy world. They will however require application, motivation and thinking about. The time invested in productive planning and creative thinking will ensure that, when it is time for action, that action will produce results.

Nevertheless, the planning and analysis described above is only of value if it leads to action. Professionals whose client work demands total accuracy and comprehensive information often look for the same when planning business development. If we wait for a 100 per cent plan, we will always be too late. Often, planning descends into 'analysis paralysis' which in turn masks a reluctance to get going.

To avoid this, each professional should be measured on the development of and implementation of a planned campaign. We should be questioning: Is it happening? Is it happening to time? Are the best tactics being used? Ultimately, did it succeed? It is better to proceed with a 70 per cent or 80 per cent plan which we amend as the plot develops.

The chapter covers three elements:

- Strategic considerations
- Managing the decision-making process
- Planning and carrying out the best tactics

STRATEGIC CONSIDERATIONS

Many textbooks draw parallels between sales and marketing strategies and military strategy. While this is sometimes taken too far we have seen that those firms who understand the principles of winning in war and can apply these principles to winning clients, have enjoyed tremendous success. We will use military analogies, sparingly, in the following discussions on how to decide the best strategy to win a significant targeted prospect.

A successful attack strategy will be based on three concepts:
- Concentration of firepower
- Attacking the competitor where he is weakest
- Timely, comprehensive and accurate intelligence

Concentration of firepower

Imagine a battle in which a heavily defended fortress sits on the top of a hill surrounded by treacherous terrain for which the attacking army have no maps. This fortress is a very important prize and needs to be taken for the attackers to achieve their ultimate objective. It would be stupid of the army commander to select one soldier, arm him with a pop gun and send him off to storm the castle with the words 'Report back when you've done it!' The soldier would feel somewhat exposed. He may try because he has been told to, he may bang his head against the brick wall several times but eventually he will give up and do something more productive. (However, the reports will probably keep coming back that: 'I'm getting there - should have some results in another day/week/month/year.')

Figure 6.1: Winning strategies: the whole picture

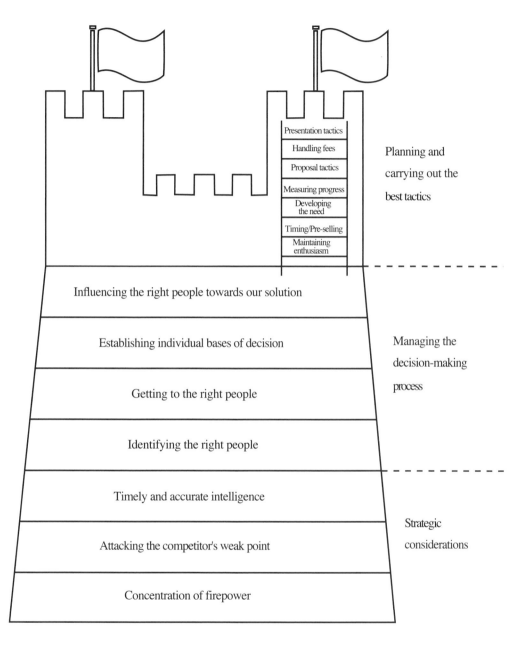

Presentation tactics
Handling fees
Proposal tactics
Measuring progress
Developing the need
Timing/Pre-selling
Maintaining enthusiasm

Planning and carrying out the best tactics

Influencing the right people towards our solution

Establishing individual bases of decision

Getting to the right people

Identifying the right people

Managing the decision-making process

Timely and accurate intelligence

Attacking the competitor's weak point

Concentration of firepower

Strategic considerations

This is exactly how a partner we know in a substantial law firm felt when he found out that he had been allocated half a dozen 'blue chip' prospects as part of the firm's 'marketing strategy'. He recognised that these prospects would make excellent clients and that his technical expertise would probably be relevant in carrying out work for them.

He was also able to secure an initial meeting with a fairly senior executive at three of the six targets.

However, as well as being very busy with fee-paying work, he found that, in each of the prospects where he managed to carry out a meeting, the incumbent legal advisers had a good reputation and a strong relationship. He felt at a loss as to how to proceed in his 'campaign'.

He was given the six targets because his firm was 'too reliant on existing clients' and had 'too few prospects'. This led to each partner being awarded six large prospects and told to get on with it. The firm had 120 well-defended fortresses in its sights and twenty partners with twenty pop guns and no time. Unsurprisingly none of these fortresses fell.

We have observed that the key to success is to concentrate effort and not spread resources too thinly even if the latter achieves the false comfort of a large prospect bank.

The principle of force

Keep the forces concentrated in an overpowering mass. The fundamental idea. Always to be aimed at before all and as far as possible.

Karl von Clausewitz

The implication is that each of the fortresses should be attacked with all available firepower a few at a time. They can be quickly overwhelmed if the attacking force is sufficiently powerful.

With regard to the law practice mentioned above this means attacking (for example) twelve prospects (not 120) with the right combination of partners and legal staff. This will help to ensure that a large proportion of those twelve become clients. This is especially important where the incumbent advisers are strong or have been in place a long time. The defenders will almost always retain control unless those looking to win the client are able to create a competitive advantage.

To create a competitive selling advantage in a professional environment, where the firm is selling its expertise and its people, requires the attacking organisation to focus the right quantity and an overwhelming quality of resource at the point in the client relationship where the incumbent competitor is weakest.

Figure 6.2: Winning strategies: strategic considerations

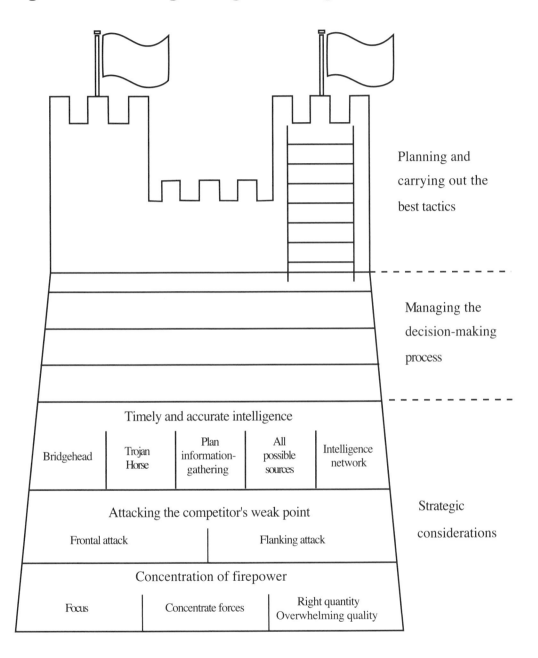

Attacking the competitor where he is weakest

> You can be sure of succeeding in your attacks if you only attack places which are undefended. *Sun Tzu (Chinese Warlord)*

There are at least two strategies we could choose from when attacking a new client.

They are:

1. *Frontal Attack* - go in with all guns blazing and try to knock the competitors out by:

- Having the best 'product'
- Having the cheapest price

2. *Flanking Attack* - identify areas of weakness in the competitor's situation, service or relationship and focus all efforts on winning in that area. This establishes a bridgehead from which to compete at a later date on more advantageous terms with the incumbent.

The latter is more likely to succeed and yet the former is almost always attempted!

For example Mark, a tax specialist confronted with a situation where a prospect is spending £100,000 every year on corporate tax advice with her existing adviser, may be tempted to compete for that work. The existing adviser has a strong relationship and has provided a good service so that although Mark and his team spend considerable time and effort on meetings, proposals, presentations and negotiations to win the assignment, the prospect eventually decides to stay where she is. The incumbent has probably had to drop his rates but this is little reward for Mark.

If, in the same scenario, Mark had explored more deeply he might have found that the prospect had one small subsidiary which imported raw materials and exported finished goods around the world. He may also have found out that the incumbent advisers had limited expertise in international taxation but were excellent on domestic issues. Then, if Mark or his team had the relevant specialist knowledge and had applied all their efforts to securing that assignment, the results might well have been different.

Instead of winning nothing, Mark would probably secure one piece of work. Mark then has the opportunity to:

- Produce excellent work which puts the incumbent to shame

- Get to know people with influence in the subsidiary and at head office

- Be in a much better position a year later to win the major taxation work as an existing adviser with a known track record and 'allies' within the client

So why do professional firms insist on going for a frontal attack? Usually because:

- The prize is so tempting it blinds them to any other options

- Everybody wants quick success, which leads to more patient approaches being discarded

- A frontal attack strategy actually means having no strategy at all. All that happens is that when an opportunity is identified everyone leaps into action

Another reason why 'full steam ahead' becomes the order of the day is that to identify the competitor's weak points and then to plan the best approach takes time, effort and skill in intelligence-gathering.

Timely, comprehensive and accurate intelligence

> Foreknowledge cannot be elicited from spirits; it cannot be obtained
> inductively from experience, nor by any deductive calculation. Knowledge
> of the enemy's dispositions can only be obtained from other men. *Sun Tzu*

In any war the most important commodity is intelligence. Spies (or spy satellites) produce information on the terrain, the defences and the opposition's movements. This intelligence dramatically influences a commander's choice of action. With superior intelligence one can almost always 'outwit' the opposition.

In exactly the same way if, after one meeting, we believe we know enough about a prospect to launch a successful attack we will be fooling ourselves. On our programmes, when participants are sceptical or bemoan the time taken on information gathering we ask them to think about their own, usually large, organisation. We ask them to think what would happen if their firm was considering a purchase which was expensive, impacted on several departments and would have a considerable impact on the bottom line of the organisation. Then we ask them to think through the discussions and meetings, the 'fors and againsts', the 'politics' and the stumbling blocks that would be involved in such a purchase. We ask them to think about the people who would have a lot of influence and others who only thought they would!

Participants often describe a tortuous process - if they actually know. This (less than perfect) understanding comes from 'living' in the firm for several years. How can this insight possibly be gained in one or two meetings? And yet having this insight (in effect a map of the terrain and a knowledge of the correct paths and the dead ends) is often the difference between success and failure. It is also very obvious from this discussion that attempting to win a significant piece of work from a new client without having met people in the client organisation - and some people do still pitch/propose blind - is a recipe for a very low conversion rate unless we have an unbeatable product, a very low price or an enormous amount of luck.

This is one obvious reason why the incumbent, if he keeps an up-to-date knowledge of the client and any changes in people and priorities, is in a favoured position. He should know which buttons to press and whose support to enlist.

Generally after one meeting we will have managed to train a spotlight onto a small part of the organisation with the rest remaining a dark hinterland. How do we bathe the rest of the terrain in strong floodlights?

Gathering intelligence

Secure a 'bridgehead' assignment

As discussed above, secure a small assignment as a bridgehead and make sure the opportunity is used to talk to, and more importantly listen to, anybody and everybody who may have useful information.

Consider a 'Trojan Horse' strategy

A Trojan Horse strategy offers the prospect a service of value to them - at no cost. For example an accountancy firm may offer to spend a couple of days helping to train the financial controller's staff in their use of accountancy software in order to increase the efficiency of the department or a law firm may offer one of their junior lawyers on secondment for a period of time. This service should not be described as 'free' but as an investment of time in establishing a relationship.

The quid pro quo provided by the client is the opportunity for us to penetrate parts of their organisation which otherwise would be unreachable. In this example it could include accounting staff, IT staff and senior managers in other functions who receive data from - and provide data to - the finance department. If this project has value to the prospect and also enables us to shed light on the internal workings of the organisation it will generate superb intelligence upon which to plan the winning of substantial pieces of work. It may even help us to identify an opportunity for work which we never would have been able to recognise through any other process.

Plan information-gathering

Produce a thought-out, detailed plan of action which is then strictly monitored and reviewed covering:

- What information is required

- What are the information sources

- Who will do what to gather the information

- When will the actions be carried out

- How and when will the information be reported back

- Who will assemble the information

- What review meetings need to be in place to discuss the information gained, to plan further phases of the process and ultimately decide how to use the information to win.

Gather information from all possible sources

Published information
Published information is especially valuable in situations where the words give an insight into the culture, ethos and aims of the organisation. This might be in the form of reported interviews with the chief executive, press statements, report and accounts, websites and company literature.

Sources inside our own firm
Very often much of the information we need is known by a selection of people who work alongside us. Some of our colleagues may have had dealings with key people in the prospect in 'past lives'. Some may have personal friends or past colleagues working for the prospect.

Some people may know somebody who knows somebody who knows somebody. It is a crime not to tap this rich source of insight by at least making it easy for anyone to come forward and be 'drained' of all potentially useful information. In our experience, especially in large firms, this is a trick that is missed.

Last year when speaking to a group of managers from a remote regional office the subject of a high profile bid recently lost by the London practice came up. The reaction from one of the group was 'If they'd asked me I could have told them what to do - I know the chap who is the assistant to the Director who made the decision. I didn't even know they were going for that company.'

At a key client meeting we were facilitating for a law firm we witnessed one of the junior lawyers mentioning for the first time that she had been seconded to the chosen key client when she was at the law firm she left six months before. The quality of the discussion improved immeasurably from that point.

Other suppliers to the prospect
We often have contacts with people who work for complementary suppliers who have already won business from this prospect. How did they do it? Could this information be of use?

'White Knights' within the prospect
Most importantly we should aim to develop an intelligence network within the prospect organisation. The aim is to have as many people as possible in different positions who are able to provide an all-round view of the situation - almost a 3D map of the terrain. From these people we would like to know:

• Answers to all the Commercial Questions described in Chapter Four

• The competition's strengths and weaknesses in the eyes of the decision-makers

• Our perceived strengths and weaknesses

• How we are doing

• What our next steps should be and anything else which helps us on our way

But why should somebody in the prospect organisation provide us with all of this information?

There are two reasons:
Reason 1 - someone on our side has a relationship with the person. This may have stemmed from an earlier business relationship or from contact at conferences, seminars, institution meetings etc. These relationships are the most useful because they are in place before the campaign to win this client begins. The information can therefore be used at an early stage of planning and can help to ensure that we follow the right track from the start. If the firm is to be in this position in as many situations as possible then:

• Everyone in the firm should be active in building potentially useful relationships with as many people working in the firm's target markets as possible. This activity, while never appearing to be urgent, is tremendously profitable in the longer term as the firm builds a network of contacts ready for 'activating' at the appropriate moment

• The knowledge of 'who knows whom' should be assembled and co-ordinated so that it is to hand when needed

*Reason 2 - he or she **wants us to win**.* This may stem from a relationship described above and may be in place before the start of the selling campaign. Alternatively, as the campaign progresses and we meet a number of people whom the decision will affect, we convince some of them that our approach, expertise or solution will be the one which benefits them or their department and in doing so we enlist them to our cause.

We will explore this process in more detail below. It is sufficient to say that if many people want us to succeed and we make use of that motivation in a professional manner, we should have a wonderful source of accurate information about both the 'hard' facts and the 'soft' issues in the prospective client's organisation.

At this point the terrain becomes floodlit, the best paths become clear, the competitor's strengths and weaknesses are obvious and we can:

- Decide on the best strategy

- Plan the correct tactics

- Concentrate our firepower

- Go on to win the prospect!

MANAGING THE DECISION-MAKING PROCESS

In a simple world the prospect's decision to purchase our services would be made by one person sifting through the facts and deciding on the best solution. In that case we would need only to identify who that person was and arrange to go and convince her of the reasons she should choose us.

Life - and sizeable prospects - are, however, not like that. Once again we should consider how important decisions are made in our firm.

If we think about the ebb and flow of influence, the different people involved, the people who are consulted - and those who are not - and the motivations behind each person's contribution, it becomes obvious that managing the decision-making process in a client or prospect requires a lot of thought and a planned approach.

Figure 6.3: Winning strategies: managing the decision-making process

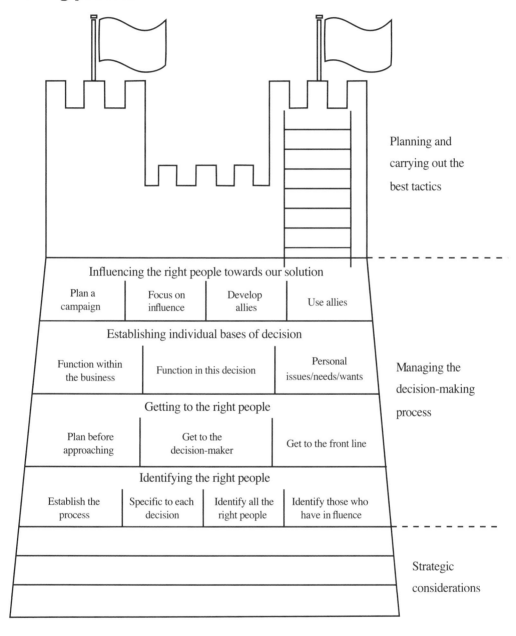

In managing the decision-making process our objective is:

To motivate all of those who will influence the decision towards our solution.

Ideally everyone should be influenced directly through one-to-one meetings. Once again it is clear that pursuing the 'one meeting then a proposal' strategy with prospects will not work.

If we are to influence the right people we need to:

- Identify who they are
- Get to them
- Establish their individual bases of decision
- Plan to influence them

Identifying the right people

In Section 3, Chapter 4 we spent some time examining the Commercial Funnels in the funnelling process. If we are able to gain an accurate understanding of those particular funnels we will be some way towards identifying the right people. We recommend that early on, and at every stage of the sale, the prospect is encouraged to discuss in detail the process involved in making this decision and to identify who will be making a contribution. You will note that this does not mean asking, 'Are you the decision-maker?' This is like saying 'Do you write the cheques around here mate?' and is likely to get a defensive, inaccurate and incomplete response.

Assuming we have established a rapport, developed credibility and asked our questions in the right way we should build an accurate picture as our contacts see it.

We need to know:

- Who will make the final decision
- Who will be affected by the purchase and will be consulted in the process
- Who has specialist knowledge and will therefore have an input
- Who will screen out bidders at different stages of the process
- Who may be consulted by the decision-maker and influencers although they are not specifically affected by this decision
- Any others whose influence could sway the decision

Several issues make this process more difficult (see below).

Identifying the right people - a potential minefield

Problem 1
Sometimes an individual says (or even believes) that she is the ultimate decision-maker but when the chips are down we find that someone else overrides the decision and decides to go with a competitor who has been selling to them.

Solution 1
By questioning carefully we must ensure that our contact doesn't feel their status is being challenged. This might lead to them overstating their authority.

Find out from other sources in the prospect their view of who the ultimate decision-maker is. Explore the process the decision will take in order to identify any final stages which have not been explained.

Problem 2
We have experience with this client or others like them which leads to incorrect assumptions about who will be involved and their level of influence.

Solution 2

The decision-making process varies between prospects. This depends on the culture of the organisation (e.g. democratic, centralised, devolved etc.) and their past experience of this type of purchase. It may also change over time.

If last year the Managing Director was the ultimate decision-maker then this year, having had experience of purchasing this type of service, she may well devolve responsibility to the Finance Director, even if the size of the budget has increased.

Conversely, if economic conditions worsen Managing Directors start to count paperclips! In this case the responsibility for certain levels of decision-making will tend to move up the organisation.

We should never make assumptions based on past experience. We must always find out how this decision will be made and keep up to date with any changes in the process as it progresses.

We cannot assume that the ultimate decision-maker is always the most senior executive but, conversely, we should not accept that the decision rests at a lower level just because the right person (e.g. the Chief Executive) is difficult to reach. We must use our contacts in the client organisation to ensure our understanding is correct.

Problem 3

We establish the 'important' decision influencers but forget about the people who will be affected day to day such as:

- The clerks in the finance department for general accountancy work
- The factory workers, supervisors and shift managers for a re-engineering project
- The salespeople when discussing a training programme

In some organisations these people will have no influence on the decision. In many others, however, their views will be canvassed. Picture the scene in a manufacturing company coming to the final decision on employing consultants to improve quality of production.

Managing Director:	'Well I think it boils down to two alternatives. They both appear fine to me. Any views Fred?'
Production Manager:	'Not really George, I think both of these outfits understand our business and have a very good track record. I did speak to the lads this morning and Joe, in the finishing shop, mentioned that the consultants from Cambridge had spent some time with him. He was impressed that they seemed down to earth and were willing to listen. I think they allayed some of his fears.'
Managing Director:	'That's useful. OK let's go with them then.'

The dialogue may seem fanciful but we have seen many important decisions turn on very small factors for and against. As companies become more democratic the people in the know (i.e. at grass roots) are likely to be consulted more and more.

Solution 3

Everyone affected by the decision must be identified and as many as possible influenced.

Even if these people are not consulted by their superiors before the decision, we may find they are lining up to sabotage our efforts if they have been convinced by one of our competitors and not by us.

We will discuss how to get to them in the next section.

Problem 4

The organisation chart can lie! People with grand, and seemingly relevant jobs and titles may turn out to have little influence. Others lower down the organisation, and perhaps to one side, end up having a major influence on how the ultimate decision-maker decides.

There is a distinction between INFLUENCE and AUTHORITY. Authority is obvious from titles and organisation charts. Influence is invisible until it has been used. We need to understand where the influence lies.

Many a contract has been lost by the selling firm identifying the wrong horse to back - the outcome is usually a cry of 'Foul' or 'It's not fair - we lost because of politics.'

Solution 4

We must know who has, and will have, INFLUENCE on this decision. In most cases this insight needs to come from people within the prospect organisation, or others who know it very well. Excellent questioning of our contacts will help.

'Who has an interest in the results of this project?'

'Who will you or the MD consult before deciding?'

'Who are the people whose views will carry greatest weight?'

The most productive source will, however, be those of our contacts who want us to win. These people can be asked even more searching questions.

'Who has X's (the decision-maker's) ear?'

'Who does X sit next to at lunch?'

'Who tends to get her way in the organisation?'

'Whose opinion will be discounted?'

'Who, in this group, is seen to be weak, out of date or out of favour?'

The answers to these questions will allow us to overlay our understanding of influence on our knowledge of the organisation structure. This will give us the real lie of the land upon which to plan the use of our resources to greatest effect.

Identifying the right people - footnote

Unless we know who the 'right' people are, all the high-powered selling resource in the world is not going to win us the client. An accurate understanding, however, will give us an excellent chance of winning. To do this we need:

• Excellent information-gathering (funnelling) skills

• As many 'allies' as possible feeding us accurate information at the right time

Getting to the right people

Plan your initial approach

Most of us have found ourselves in the position where we are blocked from getting to some key influencers, and very often the decision-maker herself, by the first person we contact in the prospect organisation. This may happen because he wants to 'keep control', because he overestimates his own power or because we haven't gained enough credibility for him to be comfortable in introducing us to others. Most often we will be fighting a losing battle here by relying on him to press our case or by trying to influence others at arm's length.

Many participants on our training programmes ask us for advice on how to get out of this situation.

The problem is that any course of action at this stage has risks attached - either in losing the business or in alienating our contact. The only real advice is not to get into the position in the first place!

At one level this means handling the initial meeting so well that our contact is keen to allow us to penetrate all and any parts of the organisation we want. We would do this by building credibility, by posing no threat to this person or their position and by 'selling' them on the benefits of our meeting all the key people. The skills involved in achieving this have been examined in Section Three.

At a more fundamental level should this person have been our first point of contact at all? It is easier to slide down an organisation than to climb up, so should we have gone in higher to start? With some insight into the people concerned could we have known that this person would be a 'blocker' and therefore have planned to meet them later in the process once we have built a relationship with others in the organisation?

Too often professionals get themselves in this extremely frustrating position because:

- They take the route of least resistance and 'see the people who will see them'

- They do not gather intelligence before making the approach

The route of least resistance often means:

1. Identifying a likely prospect.

2. Picking out someone whose title appears 'about right'.

3. Making contact with him in the way which feels most comfortable.

4. Taking it from there!

If the prospect is worth winning, it is worth investing time in research beforehand. Ideally we should get some insight into the decision-making process of the prospect before making the first approach. We should do this by exploiting all possible sources of information in the marketplace, our own firm and in the prospect organisation itself.

It may be time-consuming but not as time-consuming as a series of prospective client meetings that go nowhere. If our information is very limited then our guiding principle should be that the first point of contact should be higher than necessary rather than lower.

Getting to the decision-maker

While the decision-maker should not be the only focus of our activity it is critical that we get her on our side. It is risky to rely on others in her organisation to make our case for us. The decision-maker can also give us insight that others cannot.

If it is appropriate to make the decision-maker the first point of contact then first she must be identified and secondly persuaded that it is worth her while meeting with us. There are a large number of tried and tested ideas on how to do this successfully in one of our other publications, *Growing Your Client Base*.

A final thought. Professionals often aim too low in the target organisation. They are happier working with Technical Directors or perhaps Finance Directors who 'talk their language'. To sell effectively in today's environment however, the professional needs the skills and the confidence to add value to a meeting with people at every level. If we can't, and our competitors can, we will always be at a disadvantage.

Getting to the front line

In our earlier scenario, Joe from the finishing shop was instrumental in a decision which may have related to a million-pound purchase of consultancy services. That won't always be the case but an army of supporters is far better than an army supporting the opposition. Sometimes those who will be working with the results of our actions need to feel that they have been listened to.

If we show that we are listening, if we can meet them and demonstrate that we are human, practical and understand their problems and if we can start to develop a relationship with them we will be much more likely to win the business. We will also be more likely to enjoy their co-operation when doing the work later. But, if there is one decision-maker and a handful of senior influencers there may be tens or hundreds at 'lower' levels. How can we possibly get to them?

Step one	We 'sell' the idea of our meeting them to our existing contacts who are then keen for it to happen.
Step two	We decide who to see. A representative sample or a particular department may be sufficient. People in these groups will pass on the message to others. The more we want the business, the more people we will see.
Step three	We decide on the appropriate resource from within our organisation at every level. For example the Senior Partner for the Managing Director, other Partners for the senior executives and managers and seniors to be in contact with the front line troops.
Step four	We execute the plan. This may involve interviews, group discussions, seminars or factory visits. A Trojan Horse project may also be appropriate here.

We have now identified those people who will influence the decision. We also have plans to get in front of the right people. The next part of the jigsaw concerns how to understand the basis on which each person will influence the decision so that we can then plan to move them toward recommending us.

Establishing individual bases of decision

Our objective throughout this process is to 'motivate all of those who will influence the decision towards our solution'. When we have identified the right people, and have been successful in reaching them, our next aim is to convince each of them of the merits of our case. As discussed in Sections 2 and 3 we can only motivate someone if we understand their perceived needs, real needs and wants and the basis upon which they will make their decision.

In essence, rather than exploring and influencing one iceberg, the task now is to explore and understand a sea full of icebergs of different shapes and sizes. Just as it is inappropriate to present the same message to different clients it is also inappropriate to have one line of motivation for each person involved in the decision-making process.

There is obviously a need for consistency of message but within that general approach each person needs to be sold to differently. For example, consider a situation with two key decision influencers where one is by nature cautious and keen for the project not to fail and the other is keen to use the most creative solution and for the project to be very high profile.

Both of these people need to be convinced. All it may require is that in discussions with the former the professional stresses his firm's track record, the number of this type of project his firm has carried out and the fail-safe mechanisms in place to make sure it is delivered successfully. These points, however, would not interest the latter person who will need to hear how 'state of the art' the technology is that his firm is planning to use, how creative the input will be and what impact the project will have on the business.

It is completely feasible that one project can be presented in two, or more, different ways - the key is to know what will motivate each person and then to use that insight to rally them to our cause. We need to understand in detail each person's 'iceberg'.

There are three key elements to consider for each influencer:

- What is her function within the business?

- What is her function in this decision?

- What are her individual/personal issues, needs and wants?

Function within the business

The Sales Director of a company may want to know how our solution will affect his team, the competitiveness of the company's products and services and his people's ability to beat the competition to achieve 'top line' results.

The Finance Director, on the other hand, may be more interested in the effect on costs, reporting systems and the bottom line at each operating unit.

The Managing Director may be expected to take the broad view but this will depend on his own background (finance, marketing etc.) and his ambitions for the business.

HR Directors, Technical Directors, Production Directors, Health and Safety Managers and other managers throughout the business will all have their own 'turf' which will in turn influence their views.

Obviously the title of each person is not enough information to work on. It will be necessary to explore each person's responsibilities, the issues in their department or team and, very importantly, what they are measured on. This understanding will give us part of the story.

Function in this decision

While the influencers' input will depend in part on their responsibilities within the organisation, they may also have a specific input relating to this particular decision.

1. The decision-maker's function will be to make the final decision with more or less input from others depending on her management style and on the circumstances. If the decision-maker is responsible for the bottom line and future development of an organisation or a business unit she will make her decision based on how each proposed solution affects the present or future success of the business.

2. One or more influencers may be responsible to the decision-maker for ensuring that all proposals are up to standard and meet whatever specifications are set down. These people need to be convinced that the bid or proposal is compliant.

3. The people in the business who will be affected day-to-day by the purchase (for example the front line troops, their managers and others in affected departments) may well be giving input into the decision.

    Their function is to consider how each solution will affect them in carrying out their work. Their advice will focus on how each proposal affects their ability to perform their tasks - in terms of speed, quality etc. They will also consider personally how it makes their jobs more interesting, productive, rewarding, safe or easy to do. As noted earlier these people tend nowadays to have more and more influence and yet are the people most frequently ignored by sellers.

The three categories described above represent the roles people play. Different people will play different roles in different decisions. It is fatal to assume that we know who will play the roles based on past experience. Each decision requires investigation to find out who will be doing what in this instance.

Some people may play more than one role at a time. For example the decision-maker (1) may also be affected day-to-day by the decision (3) or one of those on the front line (3) may also be given responsibility for checking compliance (2).

There may be others in the process who do not fit neatly into the categories described above. Outside consultants may have an advisory role or a general manager from an unrelated department may be asked for advice by the decision-maker because she respects his thinking. Someone else in the business may be asked to contribute because they have specific experience or specialist knowledge.

We should beware of trying to force these people into boxes. It is important to understand for each of these very influential people:

*   What their role is in this decision
*   What they need to know to support our case
*   How we can put information across to them in the most convincing way

This final question brings us to the person rather than the role.

Personal issues/needs/wants

The iceberg principle has been explained fully in Section 2. In managing the decision-making process we need to bring all of our skills to bear to gain a real insight into each person's 'iceberg'. With the opportunity to meet each of them we can question, listen and funnel to understand what makes each of them tick.

We need to know for each person their individual:

- Ambitions
- Fears
- Concerns
- Prejudices
- Past experience
- Issues
- Motivations
- Relationships with others
- Views of the project, us, the competition
- And much more

If we are unable to meet some of the key influencers we should gain what insight we can from our allies into what makes these people tick. When we gain an accurate understanding of:

- What makes each person tick
- What role they will play in this decision
- What function they perform in the business

we will be in a position to plan what to say to each of them to motivate them towards us and our solution.

Influencing the right people towards our solution

We may need to influence two or three people or, in a major opportunity, dozens.

Whichever is relevant we need a campaign planned at the start of our approach and modified as our understanding of the prospect improves.

- This campaign plan should include an analysis of the decision-making process in all its facets described above

- Based on this analysis we need to decide on who has more or less influence and who is more or less open to our ideas. This should determine the order in which we plan to see people

- The whole campaign should be directed towards making use of any allies already in place and developing as many of the right allies as quickly as possible early in the campaign

Who are the 'right' allies? As we mentioned earlier we clearly do not want people vociferously supporting us who are regarded badly by their colleagues. We do however want to enlist those who have great influence in appropriately high places and who have an interest in the outcome of this decision. These are powerful allies. Ultimately the most powerful ally of all is the decision-maker. If she is keen for us to win and her trusted advisers agree, we are in the strongest possible position.

- Allies are developed by convincing them of the merits of our solution in their terms - personally, departmentally and in relation to their role in this decision.
  It is in this situation where professionals who are very 'technically' orientated make the mistake of presenting their solution in terms of the technical issues to everyone in the decision-making process. While this may be appropriate for those with a responsibility for screening out proposals on the basis of technical suitability it will be counter-productive for those whose interests are in either the bottom line of the business or in how it affects their day-to-day work. These people need to hear about the benefits to them of our proposals

- It is clear that the success of the campaign relies heavily on two things:
  - The 'intelligence network' and team of allies which are in place or which can be developed
  - Our skills at understanding, motivating and gaining credibility with different types of people with different motivations

An example of a tool we have developed to help a number of our clients analyse and manage the decision making process in major new targets is shown below. With the strategic plan in place the next stage will be to decide upon and implement the best tactics.

Figure 6.4 Engaging with multiple stakeholders and Influencers

Different people - different priorities

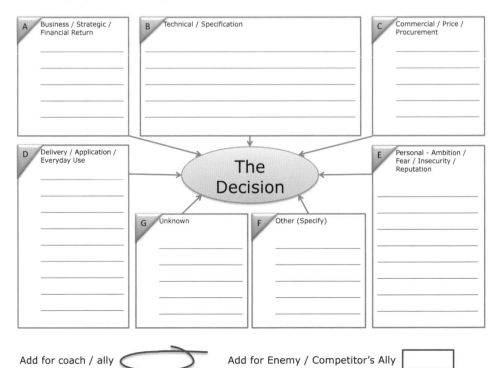

Add for coach / ally   Add for Enemy / Competitor's Ally

Figure 6.4 continued - Engaging with multiple stakeholders and Influencers

Project / Decision: _____ All Players / Stakeholders and their Priorities – Action Plan

Name	Bases of Decision							Key priorities	Coach / Ally (✓)	Level of Influence (1-10)	View of us (-5 to +5)	Actions - Who, What, When
	A	B	C	D	E	F	G					

A = Business, Financial Return, Strategic	B = Technical Specification	C = Commercial, Procurement	D = Delivery, Use, Day to Day	E = Personal - Security, Reputation, Ambition etc.	F = Other	G = Unknown

PLANNING AND CARRYING OUT THE BEST TACTICS

The plans and strategies have been developed. Now the professional has to carry them out successfully. The focus is on winning! Coming 'second' gets no prizes. Now is the time to invest the appropriate energy and resources to make sure that we are successful. This section concentrates on how to carry our plans through. However, before we consider how best to manage the process, let us consider the situations where our freedom of movement is limited.

Situations where the process is dictated to us

Some of our clients tell us that they have no control over the buying process once a bid is being pursued. For example in a sizeable public sector project the client may strictly define the specification and limit the actions allowed by the selling organisation and its personnel. In these situations the winner will be the organisation which has the 'best' solution or the cheapest price or both. If the approach is totally dictated by the buying organisation there is no opportunity to 'sell'. However, we would give the following guidance.

There are only a few situations where there is no freedom of movement

Very often we limit ourselves by not exploring and challenging the process in detail. We do not 'sell' the client on the benefits she will derive from a more flexible approach. The unpalatable truth is that if we are reliant on these very restricted situations our work will be at very low margins or even loss-making unless we are significantly more efficient than our competitors. If the margins are low then it is even more imperative for us to secure work in other buying situations where greater flexibility allows us to put forward a better case and to command reasonable rates.

Stretch the rules where possible

Where there is some flexibility we would recommend stretching the rules as far as possible without alienating any members of the decision-making process. In that case we should select some of the ideas outlined below and try them out - see how far we can go and what advantage that brings us.

Build relationships early

If our freedom of manoeuvre is limited once the bidding process starts, but the prospect has some discretion in purchasing, then our chances will depend on the relationships we have built up before the project becomes 'live'. This in turn depends on using the strategies and tactics described in this section both to get on the tender list and to give ourselves an advantage over the competition once there.

In situations where there is a flexible process, or no defined process at all, we must take advantage of the situation to ensure we win. If we have selected the right strategy, gathered intelligence and at least started to understand the decision-making process then the following tactics will help us to move from first contact to ultimate success.

Figure 6.5 Winning strategies: planning and carrying out the best tactics

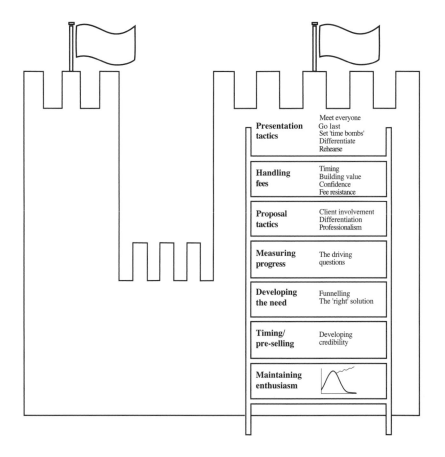

Maintaining enthusiasm

Figure 6.6 represents a situation faced by many professionals.

Imagine a speculative first meeting with a prospective client. This prospect has enough interest to agree to a meeting - represented at point 1 in Figure 6.6. The meeting itself goes extremely well. We develop great rapport and compatibility, gain a high level of credibility and demonstrate competence. We also get to understand and agree some issues critical to the business which need to be addressed and put forward some ideas with which the prospect is highly impressed. We stay for two hours when we originally expected 40 minutes.

The prospect not only takes us back to reception but walks with us back to the car saying, 'I am very impressed. I know that you could bring added value to the organisation and, besides, our existing consultants are far too complacent. We are going to need to talk in detail about this in a couple of months, at which point I'll call you in to meet the MD so that we can get you appointed.'

Figure 6.6 How enthusiam drops

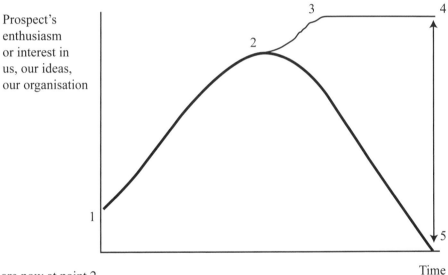

We are now at point 2.

As we float on air back to the office we think that perhaps business development is not so bad after all. We go to see the Senior Partner and describe the situation in glowing terms, in fact we probably remember an even more positive situation than we actually heard - maybe up to point 3.

We drop the prospective client a line to thank her for the meeting and wait for her to call. Eight weeks pass and we start to watch the phone. At ten weeks we are a little disappointed but she did say 'a couple of months' and these things do tend to get delayed. At twelve weeks we wonder whether to phone but we don't want to pester her. At fourteen weeks the Senior Partner is getting on our back because this organisation has been on our list of good prospects for months now. Eventually at sixteen weeks we pluck up the courage and ring her:

Professional	Good morning, Janet, it's Peter Smith from CBD.
Client	Er... hello.
Professional	Hello.
	I hope you don't mind but I was ringing to follow up our meeting in January.
Client	Umm... remind me.
Professional	Oh sure! We were talking about ways of providing some creative solutions to the problems you were having in France and Germany.
Client	Oh. Right. What was the name again?
Professional	Peter.
Client	Oh yes. Peter remind me, how did we leave our discussions?
Professional	You were going to phone me so that I could come in and meet the MD to discuss what we could do.
Client	I remember now. As it happens the issues in France and Germany came to a head three weeks ago. We had to get some quick solutions so Jim arranged for our existing consultants to go over and recommend some changes. They've just produced their draft report. I am still interested in talking to you when other issues arise, but it would probably not be appropriate to meet now. Look, please keep in touch, I would be interested to hear of any developments.
Professional	Oh, sure, OK.
Client	Thanks for phoning. Goodbye.

One thing is for certain here. The client's level of interest, let alone memory of the meeting, was a lot lower than the professional expected! The professional has a memory of the meeting which has not changed in the intervening weeks (now at point 4) while, for whatever reasons, the prospect's enthusiasm has reduced dramatically to point 5. Why the drop? Perhaps the story goes something like this:

- As soon as the prospect got back to her office the MD came in with a rush job to do by Monday

- On Monday she learnt that she would have to present the findings to the worldwide board and one of her most trusted subordinates handed in his resignation

- During the next week a fault in the computer system created havoc in her department, she learned that her best friend had had her first baby (and a letter arrived from Peter thanking her for a meeting last week)

- Over the next two weeks the firm secured a large order, decided to move to new premises and narrowly averted a strike in its Spanish factory

- In the next month things really went mad at work, she was working 70 hours a week and, partly because of this, her husband left her for his secretary etc. etc

In other words there have been more things on her mind than the meeting we remember so vividly. No wonder four months later she couldn't remember us, let alone the meeting.

The diagram should focus our minds on one simple aim - to maintain and develop the prospect's level of enthusiasm so that it is as high as possible at the right time. In this situation the professional's principal task is to ensure that the level of interest follows line (a) not line (b).

When an issue becomes current we must be right at the front of her mind and not a distant memory. How can we do this?

Figure 6.7 Maintaining enthusiasm

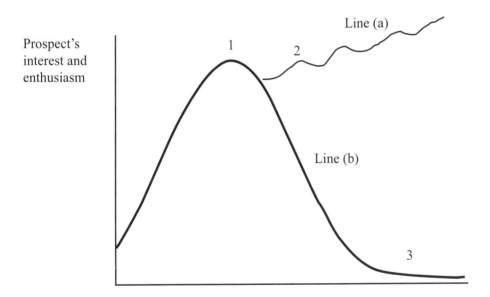

Maintain telephone contact

At the end of the meeting we could explain to her that we would like to consider the information we have gained and that if we have any further queries on the detail we may ring her in the next few days. She is enthusiastic at this stage and will always say 'Yes'. We should then ring her - even if there are no real gaps in our information - we can ask a couple of questions and take the opportunity to remind her of the things that made her enthusiastic at the meeting.

Email

We can email her three to four days after our phone call. This email does not just thank her for the time, it also summarises the key issues she faces and the things she liked about how we might approach such a situation.

Meet with other people

Other interested parties may have been identified during the meeting. We should ask to see them early rather than wait for any project to be 'live'. In this way their views can be taken into account. Timing is key - we should ask her at a time when she is likely to say 'Yes'. This is when her enthusiasm is high - in Figure 6.7 at point 1 or 2 and not point 3 a month later when her interest has died down.

Keep in contact

When we have seen others in the decision-making process we need to feed back information to the initial contact and take the opportunity to remind her of the benefits we can bring. Throughout this time we should also be engaging with this client through the most appropriate and effective social media channels.

Demonstrate that we are showing interest

We can sustain motivation by sending thought pieces and articles of our own, cutting out and sending other people's articles and information which would interest her, even if they are not directly relevant to our area of expertise, inviting her to relevant seminars and conferences, inviting her to the kind of hospitality events we know she would like to attend and contacting her at appropriate intervals to touch base. However, at all times remember that all of this contact must be of relevance - valuable, interesting, fun or all of these. Anything we do or send that is irrelevant only demonstrates that we either do not understand her or we do not care enough to make sure we do not waste her time. *Anything that is not positive is not neutral it is negative* - it speeds up the rate at which her enthusiasm will decline.

Agree the contact frequency

Many professionals are afraid of 'pestering' prospects, so they go to the other extreme and let these contacts drift. This can easily be avoided by agreeing the frequency of contact with the prospect. Remember: we must have this discussion at a point where the 'interest curve' is high. We should also make the responsibility for making the contact ours, not hers.

Test commitment

As well as building commitment we should be checking it. It is easy to be deluded by polite prospects who make us feel better by projecting more enthusiasm than they feel. As discussed in Chapter Five, commitment involves the client in action. We can ask her to do something which will take a little time - e.g. send us some information - and if it does not arrive, question what interest really exists.

Involve the prospect in developing the need See below.

Involve the prospect in the design and presentation of the solution
See below.

We hear of many more ways of sustaining enthusiasm used by professionals each day.

The key is to understand that this is the aim of this part of the campaign and then to do anything to keep that curve going up.

Getting the timing right

There is a natural tendency in many of us either to move too quickly when there is a large prize in sight or alternatively to show how service-orientated we are by responding with solutions at the earliest possible time. If we succumb to these instincts we put ourselves at a disadvantage.

Figure 6.8 represents a situation where there is a time lag between first contact with a prospect and a decision to buy a specific service.

In this situation the right time to put forward our solutions is as close to decision date as possible, e.g. at point 1. Note: this assumes we have explored the commercial funnels and that we know the final decision date.

Figure 6.8 Timing our proposals

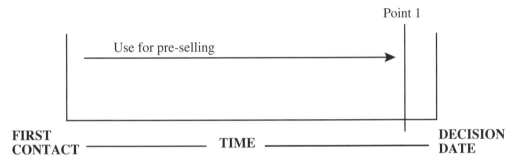

Why so late?

- If we put forward our ideas earlier the prospect can pass them on to others to see if they can do them more cheaply and she can also consider doing the work in-house

- Alternatively if we give ourselves more time for gaining a comprehensive understanding of the requirements, issues and politics of the situation the solution is more likely to be right and acceptable to all

- If we have some radical, and positive, ideas which change the situation materially the tendency is to communicate them to the prospect as soon as we think of them. This enables them to be passed on and tried out by others. However, if the prospect hears these radical ideas within a day or two of the decision date she has to decide in favour of our solution if she wants the benefits which these ideas deliver. This is especially powerful if we are trying to 'pull the rug' from underneath an incumbent firm

- The more time we have between first contact and proposal the more time we have for 'pre-selling' and credibility building

What is pre-selling?

In many competitive situations the people in the decision-making process have almost made up their minds who they will choose before they see the presentations or proposals! They know who they want to win and as long as that firm puts forward a credible solution in line with their expectations they will vote for them. The other competitors are there to make up numbers.

This does not mean that the presentation or proposal should not be first class. What it does mean is that we should ensure that our proposition is the one they are looking forward to and expecting to win. To this end we should invest as much energy as possible in the pre-selling phase, building up credibility and persuading the relevant people that we are the organisation they will want to work with.

David Maister in his article 'How Clients Choose' supports our conclusions. He says: "The vast majority of professional projects are awarded at the pre-proposal stage: the formal proposal and/or presentation merely confirm (or destroy) a decision already made. If you can't afford to spend time up-front, don't bother writing the proposal".

There are a number of actions we can take to develop credibility, build compatibility, demonstrate competence and place us in a strong tactical position in the month, quarter or even six months between first contact and final presentation of the solution.

For example we can:

- Ensure we meet with (all of) the people who will have influence on the future decision

- Introduce some new ideas which could become an integral part of the required solution. In this way we are changing the position of the goalposts for the other competitors. They will have to play 'catch up' - if they ever find out the goalposts have been moved

- Try to find out the parts of competitors' solutions which are favoured - on the basis that some competitors will be tactically naive and submit proposals far too early

- Build alliances with third parties who may be able to offer help

- Invite key players from the prospective client to suitable hospitality events

- Carry out 'mini assignments' and 'health checks' where we can demonstrate expertise very quickly

- Invite the prospect to seminars where we can show our expertise and where she can meet our delighted clients

- Send articles and information related to her situation which underline our knowledge

- Invite her to our offices where she can meet a selection of people who will say those things which will increase our credibility

- If appropriate invite her to speak to relevant clients and possibly to meet them to see what benefits we have been able to bring to their organisations

- Provide case studies of similar projects we have carried out

- Introduce those people from our side who will actually carry out the work

- Ensure that deadlines are agreed for any correspondence, contact etc. and that they are always met

- Underpromise and overdeliver - promise to do things in an acceptable timescale and quality and then do better every time

Pre-selling is not selling our solution. It is preparing the ground for a positive response. There is no point in spending considerable time and money on the best presentation or proposal unless we are prepared to invest the time in pre-selling. Delaying the final solution to the right point gives us the time to do this.

Developing the need

The PACES process makes it clear that the time and skill invested in understanding a client's requirements through effective funnelling forms the basis of a successful sale. It is true also that being 'funnelled' helps the client to consider her own perceived needs, real needs and wants more deeply.

To win significant new prospects the professional must ensure that all the key members involved in the decision-making process have been through this degree of 'soul searching'. They must not only understand the perceived needs. They must also understand:

- The real needs (if at variance to the perceived needs)
- The wider implications
- The short- and long-term effects
- The wants of people that may also have to be met
- The effects on others
- The relationship to corporate and departmental business objectives
- The implications if things go wrong, are delayed, incomplete etc
- The relative importance of each element of the needs
- The specific elements of the professional's expertise which are critical to the success of the assignment

If these elements are not understood in some depth by the key people within the client, they will believe that the need is very 'simple' and relatively easy to meet. This will mean that, in the prospect's eyes, a large number of firms could meet the need adequately and the services being considered will tend to be regarded as a commodity. This is how audit work is perceived now - with the obvious effect on profitability. Many accountants are attempting to 'bolt added value' onto audits in the hope of differentiating themselves and generating more profit. This will only be successful if each prospect can be helped to see the need for these extra services and to understand the wider implications of their purchasing decisions.

It follows from the above that we should spend considerable time with decision makers and influencers getting them to understand their requirements. As discussed in earlier chapters, the fatal mistake is to try to tell the client what she needs, even if we are sure we know. The only way to help her to understand is by asking searching questions from a position of high credibility and demonstrable competence and compatibility.

The ideal outcome is for us (and the prospect) to understand the detailed requirements better than our competitors. However, even if the prospect communicates her new-found insight to our competition, we are still ahead because:

- We have already added value to the prospect
- We have developed credibility and been involved in a consultant/client relationship rather than as buyer/seller (although as yet unpaid!)
- The 'specification' as developed is likely to have our 'fingerprints' all over it
- With the requirements now being more demanding there are fewer competitors who will be able to put forward a credible solution

Finally, defining the need in greater depth and avoiding a 'too simple' solution will help to ensure that the prospect gets the right solution - one that meets her needs most closely and provides the best short- and long-term benefits. Too often prospects buy what is 'easy to buy' and regret the decision at their leisure. If we are the winners in one of these situations we may not enjoy the resulting experience and the project will almost certainly not generate the level of benefits which will help us to win more business or generate referrals.

Measuring progress

'The project is worth £200,000 and the probability of us winning is 70 per cent.' Statements like this are heard in many professional firms, often with the following limitations:

- The 70 per cent probability is pure 'gut feel'
- The £200,000 is guesswork and usually overstated
- The professional's estimates are not reviewed later to measure their accuracy
- This estimate is added together with other 'gut feels' to arrive at a forecast which appears now to be very scientific
- The focus of the discussion is on the 70 per cent supposedly achieved and not on the 30 per cent gap which needs to be filled

We have yet to find the perfect system which accurately measures the probability of winning business, especially if a relatively small number of large projects are being pursued.

However, the most important use of an accurate analysis is not to determine 'where we are' but is to aid in planning ACTIONS which will measurably reduce the gap, increase the probability figure and ultimately enable us to win the business.

The best way of measuring progress and planning forward movement is to divide the P3 Segment of the PACE Pipeline itself into four levels - Q1 to Q4. For a prospective piece of work to reach each level progress needs to have been made and a certain number of driving questions answered. These criteria and questions need to be very tough so that:

- They give a hard-nosed view on how far we have come
- It is very clear what the next set of actions should be

An example of such a framework is given on the following page:

Table 6.1: Tracking progress (DMP = Decision-making Process; USP = Unique Selling Point; BOD = Basis of Decision)

Class	Qualification criteria	The driving questions
Qualified opportunity Level 1 **Q1**	1. Opportunity identified. 2. Discussions initiated.	Have we met with at least one person who has sufficient authority to give us a clear brief of requirements?
	3. Our solution possible.	Do we know that there is a problem or opportunity (agreed by the prospect) which needs resolution? Can we address the requirements? Is our solution likely to be technically acceptable?
	4. Our type of client.	Is the prospect likely to be willing to pay for the added value areas which we typically incorporate in our solutions?
Qualified opportunity Level 2 **Q2**	1. Bases of decision understood.	Do we fully understand their current situation (e.g. structure, processes, applications, incumbent systems)?
	2. Business drivers understood.	Do we fully understand the positioning and synergy of the incumbent suppliers?
	3. Budget situation understood.	Do we know the opportunity costs of their current situation?
	4. Players, timescales and DMP understood.	As a departmental objective, how important is this project? Why?
	5. Pre-selling strategy and plan formulated.	As a corporate objective, how important is the project? Why? Do we understand the financial operations of this company? Do they have the money available? Which budget does this come from? Is the budget sufficient to cover our solution? Who is the budget-holder? Could more money be found? If so, from where? Do we know all of the players in the DMP? Who are they? Have we met them? Do we know what their roles will be? Do we know the process by which this decision will be reached? What is this? Do we know the requirements of all of the players? Has the decision-maker committed to make a decision? Do we know their timescales for agreement and implementation? Have we formulated a strategy to pursue this prospect and have we put together a pre-selling plan?

Class	Qualification criteria	The driving questions
Qualified opportunity Level 3 **Q3**	1. Short-listed competitors known.	Have we presented a solution which has been cost-justified?
	2. Financially acceptable solution.	Has the prospect dedicated time/effort/ resource to fully evaluate our solution? How has this been carried out?
	3. Talking with decision-maker and key influencers.	Has the solution been accepted and agreed by all the key players?
		Have the key players told us that they particularly like aspects of our solution? What are these aspects?
		Do we know all of the other alternatives they are considering?
		Are there no more than two other competitors still in the race?
		Do we know the offerings being made by the competitors?
		Have we created a requirement for USPs which only we can provide?
		Have our competition created a requirement for USPs which we will find difficult/impossible to provide?
		Have we got alternatives/arguments to deflect the competitors' USPs?
		If our proposal is accepted, what may the different individuals involved in the DMP have to give up?
Qualified opportunity Level 4 **Q4**	1. Verbal commitment.	Have we met the BOD of all the key players?
	2. 'Closing meeting' fixed.	Are we in a 'short list of one' with the business only subject to discussion and negotiation on final details?
	3. Paper trail understood.	Have we actually been told by the decision-maker (or her direct messenger) that we have won the business?
		Is a 'closing meeting' arranged?
		Do we understand, in detail, the client's paper trail - how, when, where and by whom the decision will be ratified from their side?
		Have we triggered the client's internal mechanism for raising a purchase agreement?
		Have we developed genuine allies?

Applying this approach to live prospects and projects in the Pipeline often leads to a number of reactions:

- Surprise at how many 70 per cent prospects are still in Q1

- Surprise at how few prospects are in Q3 or Q4

- Concern at the number of absolutely critical questions we do not have a completely rock solid answer to

By using this process one of our clients has managed to achieve an 80+ per cent conversion rate on opportunities moving between P3 and P4 of the Pipeline.

Proposal tactics

Introduction

The formal written proposal is an important part of the sales process. The ability to develop winning proposals is crucial, particularly for those who find it difficult to differentiate their products, services or 'offering' in the mind of the client. However, the proposal itself is only one element of the process of 'winning'. Another equally important aspect is the ability to use proposals effectively.

Proposals and the sales cycle

By the time a client has decided that they need a proposal from us (and perhaps the competition) they have already identified some kind of problem - or opportunity - that needs resolution. Therefore, in many cases we are already very late in the sales process.

If we can identify the prospect's problem before they do, we give ourselves the opportunity of providing our solution without the constraints that competition and alternatives often generate. Therefore we should be working with prospects to ensure that we spot problems and opportunities before they occur rather than responding to the known. We should be trying to create an edge for ourselves by approaching prospects with new ideas before their existing advisers identify them. This often highlights to the client where their existing adviser relationship has become too familiar and where they are not getting added value.

Proposals - do they really want one?

Often prospective clients ask for a proposal, 'because that's the thing to do'. If asked to provide a proposal, we need to ensure that is what the client really wants. Often this is the only mechanism they recognise to help them to make a decision. In fact research shows that competitive proposals and their follow-up often confuse the decision to be made rather than simplifying it. We should offer alternatives to a proposal that might give us an advantage. For example:

- A visit to our offices to allow the client to see and experience the unique features/ approach that only we have to offer

- A visit to see an already happy client, who will undertake some of the selling for us

- A presentation with plenty of interaction, thus allowing us to adapt our proposals more closely to the client's requirements, as we go

- A 'workshop' involving the client's decision-making team designed to stimulate plenty of discussion again allowing us to adapt our proposals more closely to the client's requirements

Before offering alternatives we should consider those areas in which we and our organisation have particular expertise. We can then build our alternative to a proposal around those strengths. This may be the only real way to differentiate ourselves from the competition.

Proposals - keeping the prospect involved

Once we have gained the opportunity to prepare a proposal, we must not retreat to our 'ivory tower' and leave the prospective client alone until it is completed. If we can ensure that the prospect's interest is stimulated during this period we have a far better chance of winning the business.

Before starting work on the proposal, we should ask the client if it is acceptable to contact her with any questions and queries that may arise. We should then plan to do so. If there is a delay between gaining the opportunity and completion of the proposal then we must phone the client, ask questions to clarify details and tell her how the proposal is developing.

Before producing the finished article it is generally a very good tactic to produce a draft copy (marked clearly DRAFT COPY), and then arrange a meeting with the client. At this meeting we should stress that we have a draft copy of the proposal and that we would like their input. One copy is enough. This ensures that both sides have to 'get together' to study the draft. Based upon our information-gathering meetings we should select the areas that were of greatest interest to the client. We then ask for her comments 'to ensure that we have understood absolutely correctly'. If she has any observations we should suggest that she makes her comments directly onto the draft proposal. All of this helps to make it her proposal not ours. If this is the case then at final proposal stage she will be looking for ways to agree with our recommendations, not to pick holes in them.

We can then make arrangements with the client to hand-deliver the final proposal, to give us the opportunity to answer any queries she may have. This creates an additional opportunity for us to develop our ideas further and is particularly useful when our proposal is the last to arrive with the client.

If there is to be a delay between giving the proposal to the client and her making a decision, we can ask for approval to 'keep in touch' during this period - and make sure that we do - but don't push!

Will the client be happy to stay involved and to contribute to the development of our proposal? Once again it will depend on how motivated she is and how much she wants us to win, i.e. how much we have managed to build her motivation to buy.

The proposal itself

It would be very easy to write a whole book on the subject of writing winning proposals - in fact a number of these books have already been written. That is not the aim of this section however we have listed below a number of keys to success that we have collected over the years:

1. Demonstrate absolute clarity of understanding of the client's requirements in the proposal.

2. Make the proposal easy to understand.

3. Focus on the interesting bits! (To the client.)

4. Include nothing that could make the client think "so what?".

5. Get ideas from past proposals but do not 'cut and paste' anything into the key sections of the proposal.

6. Do not treat any proposal as 'routine'.

7. Make sure the format is exactly right for the client.

8. Develop a process for making the most of every proposal opportunity and ensure everyone in the office / practice / firm knows the key steps and follows them.

9. Agree the length and style of proposal with the client.

10. Use colour, diagrams and pictures to ensure the client remembers the key parts of the proposal.

11. Use technology where appropriate.

12. Rewrite CVs every time to focus them on what interests the client.

Fee handling

Price versus value

In most competitive situations the fee will be a key element in the prospect's decision to buy. However, unless our service is a pure commodity, where the only difference between competitors is price, the prospect will be making a judgement concerning price and value. While the price needs to be competitive, our real efforts need to go into building value in the eyes of the client.

When to present the price

Timing is important. Everything mentioned so far in this section has been focused on increasing the prospect's motivation to buy and building her perceived value of what we do. If we are tempted - or forced - into presenting our fees before this motivation is built, the prospect may immediately dismiss us as 'too expensive'. If, however, the prospect has been so impressed by our approach, our solution and the benefits of our proposals that she starts to believe she 'cannot live without our services' before we discuss fees she will be looking for ways of justifying the price. The message is: delay presenting the price until the prospect wants to buy.

It is important to note the difference between price and budget. Price comes towards the end of the process. Budget is a factor we need to find out as early as possible so that we can tailor our solution to meet the prospect's pocket.

Determining value

The value the client puts on our solution will depend on:

- The importance of the 'problem'
- The benefits which derive from the solution
- The urgency of the need
- The number and quality of potential alternative suppliers
- The corporate and personal implications of getting the project right or wrong

How we price our work should take these factors into account. We need to establish the answers to these questions (and influence the prospective client's views) during the A and C phases of the PACES process.

Believing our pricing

The price we get will also be determined by how much we believe we, or our solution, are worth. One week before an important pitch we were observing a team of consultants preparing their presentations. When it got to discussing the fees one said: 'That looks expensive, don't you remember we lost the last one at this rate.' There was a general murmur of agreement but the partner present said: 'No - we need this fee to make this project worthwhile.' It was obvious that no one was convinced. This was not only obvious to us but also to the prospect the week after.

At the pitch the team were totally confident in their delivery up to the point they had to present the price itself. Then, for the first time, the team member responsible hesitated, shuffled, mumbled a little and lost eye contact with the audience. The decision-makers, consciously or subconsciously noted these signals and one immediately commented, 'That sounds expensive.' It was a classic 'self-fulfilling prophecy'.

This attitude is central to the profitable success of a professional who has a 'product' which may be invisible and where there is no set price. In this situation we have noticed that a major factor in deciding the rate which can be achieved is the professional's own confidence in what the solution is 'worth'. This confidence must be built. The seller needs to be convinced before the buyer can be.

Handling fee resistance

We know professionals who send in proposals to prospective clients and then wait to hear whether they have won or lost. In some selling environments there is no alternative to this. In many others, however, it is possible to have some contact with the prospect after she has examined the proposals and before she has made the decision. This gives the seller the chance to explore and handle any issues which are not exactly right. One of these issues might be the fees.

We would suggest that if it is possible to have some discussion before the decision is made then this chance must be grasped. That is not to say that we will automatically reduce the price but it does mean that if there is a 'deal' which is acceptable to both sides it can be found.

However, this situation must be handled well. It is probably the part of the process where instinct is the poorest guide. When someone says 'You're too expensive!' there are two instinctive reactions: either we start to mumble and reduce the rate easily, or we defend our rates mightily.

The latter of these sounds more productive but not if it is done like this:

Prospect	You're too expensive!
Professional	Well Ms Prospect, not when you consider what you are getting for your money. We are providing top quality staff and an excellent project manager. The technology we are using is state of the art and our people will be providing very detailed reports at each stage. I have asked our Director to take a personal interest and I will be involved on a day-to-day basis. Also...

The danger here is that the professional has started to include features which are not relevant to the client, certainly are not valuable and are only included now to defend the fee. In effect the professional is confirming the prospect's views - these unwanted features explain *why* he is too expensive. This is absolutely the wrong way to handle fee resistance.

When the prospect states we are too expensive we need to find out more:

*   What is she comparing us to?
*   What are the details of the competitive offers (as known by the prospect)? In particular have they scoped the project in the same way or built in more reliance on scarce client resources?
*   What are the competing rates?

This information may be hard to ascertain but:

*   The more the prospect wants us to win the more open she will be
*   The more allies we have in the prospect organisation the more sources of information we have
*   The more we gather and share competitor information the better we are able to estimate their rates - if necessary
*   There is much less risk in asking than in not asking

Once we have some idea of the difference in price and the difference in solutions between us and each of the variable solutions we can do the only thing possible - sell our extra benefits for the extra price we are asking. We should not resell benefits that are common to a number of alternatives - the prospect's response will be: 'I can get all that elsewhere and spend less.' We must focus on the difference.

If the extra benefits we are offering are not worth the extra price then the prospect should buy from the competition! There is no magic wand!

However, we should consider two factors:

1. We do not have to *be* better - the prospect just needs to *think* we are. For instance if we

know the competitor has everything we have to offer but their professional is poor at selling, we may still be able to convince the client of the added advantages in choosing us - and also achieve a fee premium.

2. Our extra benefits may not be worth all of the proposed difference to the client but they may be worth a proportion. In this instance it may be necessary for us to negotiate a reduction in rates but not right down to the competitor's rate. As all business managers know, the small percentages saved here add up.

Summary

Price is always likely to be an important factor in the client's decision. Our challenge is to build the value of our solution in the prospect's mind so that the potential cost of not using us outweighs any premium we can charge. This value derives from using every skill and tactic described in this book so far. If a professional is effective at selling in a consultative fashion he will not only generate more business - he will also achieve higher fee rates than others in the same profession who are less skilful or less confident.

And if we can achieve higher rates we don't have to work so hard for the same return!

Presentation tactics

Many professional firms have spent considerable amounts of money in recent years in developing their senior people's presentation skills. It seemed the obvious first step when the marketplace became more competitive and clients were arranging formal pitches and 'beauty parades' as part of the purchasing process. It should be clear from this book that the presentation is only one link in the chain and, while it is important to be able to present well, the most polished speakers will not necessarily secure the client.

Before standing up to make a pitch to one or more decision-makers and influencers the successful professional will have achieved as many of the following as humanly possible. He will have:

*   Explored all of the issues (technical, business, commercial and personal)
*   Built credibility with all of the key people present
*   Developed the need and helped to write the specification
*   Tested his solutions and gained input from the decision-makers so that these solutions are as much theirs as his
*   Understood the decision-making process and found out what each person will want to hear
*   Focused on the areas where his firm has an advantage over the competition. This information will be gleaned from the decision-makers themselves or his 'allies' in the prospect
*   Checked his understanding of the real situation through his intelligence network in the prospect
*   Focused on the issues which are closest to the hearts of the people with real INFLUENCE both in the organisation and with regard to this decision
*   Prepared the ground so that the audience are keen to hear the presentation and expect it to be the best

Once we are in this position then we should focus on presenting well. We should also employ the tactics that ensure we will win.

What tactics can we use?

Try to meet everyone beforehand

Ideally meet everyone beforehand - or at least the key decision influencers.

On the positive side this allows us to personalise the presentation to the individuals present. For instance:

> 'Fred, your key interest was in the communication process throughout the project - what we have done here is...
>
> ...while for you Joe the critical issue was in the person you would be working directly with - we would propose George because he has...
>
> ...Jane, while the areas I have covered are also very important for you, the most important consideration for your department is on Health and Safety, our plans here are... etc.'

A presentation should sound like a conversation with the audience. If we have not met them before, this is very hard to achieve.

On the negative side we have seen the risks at first hand of not meeting with all of the key people before the presentation. In one instance we took a brief from the Human Resources Director of a major plc - it was quite detailed and we felt we had a very credible solution. The presentation was to the Human Resources Director, Managing Director and Sales Director. As usual we started the presentation by summarising our understanding of the requirements. Half-way through the summary the Managing Director became restless and by the end her body language was positively hostile. We tried to find out why:

Us	Jane, you don't appear too happy - is anything not correct in the summary?
Jane	Nothing is correct. It's all wrong. That's not the situation and it's not what I came along here today to see.
Us	Which bits are you not happy about?
Jane	All of it - you clearly do not understand the issues.
Us	Alison (the Human Resources Director) - I'm sure these were the areas we discussed in some detail. Has anything changed since our last meeting?
Alison	(Backtracking madly) Oh no - I would agree with the Managing Director - I am afraid you must have misinterpreted what I said.
Us	Gulp!!

As you can imagine we did not secure the client!

Make it different

Think of different ways to present the solution. Personalise it to the client.

We have seen beauty parades where accountants spend most of their time convincing the prospect that they know how to carry out an audit and lawyers who focus on convincing the client they know the law. The clients afterwards complained that they could not tell the difference between the firms presenting and what they wanted to hear was anything special in terms of service, people, 'delivery' or added value. Make it different - the most important thing is to be remembered.

Go last

Much research shows this is the best position for most circumstances. If we go last and demonstrate real effectiveness we have the best chance of being remembered.

If we can't go last, go first

If we are presenting first we should think up one or two very difficult questions that all the presenting firms could be asked. Spend time thinking of the best answers to these questions. If at the end of the presentation the questions have not been asked we should bring them up ourselves by saying, 'One question you may be asking yourself at this point might be... the way we would handle this would be...'

The prospect is now very likely to ask this question of all of our competitors. Unlike us they only have a couple of seconds to think of a good answer. In effect we will have laid one or more time bombs to go off in our competitors' faces! Remember we are playing to win!

Practise and rehearse

Everyone knows the difference a rehearsal can make to the quality of a presentation - especially if more than one person is involved. We would recommend two or three rehearsals to get it right.

We would also recommend rehearsing the presentation with the client! Why would she agree to that? One very good reason is that if one or more people are responsible for organising the beauty parade then their credibility is at stake as much as ours - they are keen to 'get it right'. In that instance, and if we have developed a reasonable relationship with the person, we should ask whether we can 'run through what we are going to say just to make sure we have got it spot on'. (If we cannot arrange a meeting a ten-minute phone call could be invaluable.)

Our reward comes when our contact says: 'It sounds good, just two points - I think you should stress your experience with ABC Ltd a bit more - the Managing Director really admires them - and, whatever you do, reduce the "technospeak" at the beginning, that would put the Sales Director right off and he won't listen to the rest.' These tips will often mean the difference between success and failure.

Two final points:

- We might as well ask if we can rehearse with the client - there is nothing to lose
- Ensure we are talking with an accurate and well-informed source - remember Alison, the Human Resources Director mentioned earlier!

STRATEGIES THAT WIN NEW CLIENTS - SUMMARY

Winning significant new clients means achieving a balance between thought and action. It means deciding what is best, and then carrying out the appropriate plan rather than believing that hard work alone will bring the right level of reward.

To be successful the professional firm should:

- Concentrate its firepower on the right targets based on timely and accurate intelligence
- Identify, meet and influence the right people in each situation
- Plan, carry out and review the tactics at each stage of the buying process to ensure that the firm wins

If this seems like a lot of effort - it can be. Whether it is appropriate depends on one question: 'What is/will be the "lifetime value" of this prospect as a client?'

Chapter 7 **Some Final Thoughts**

In a demanding world, where clients have a choice, the professional who ignores the importance of being able to sell well runs the risk of facing a less secure future. Technical excellence – being a great engineer, accountant, lawyer, actuary etc. - is of course essential and most professionals never stop trying to be better at what they do. However, confidence and skills in selling are now more than ever prerequisites for a secure, successful and fulfilling career.

Achieving conscious competence in the skills of winning business – and applying those skills more often and better than your competitors – is critical to winning more of the right work from the right clients at the right price.

HOW TO BECOME A GREAT PERFORMER

There are two steps to effectively developing any skill to a high level. The learner has to first of all understand what it is that he is trying to achieve - someone has to delineate the skill. As a novice golfer this could be achieved by reading a book on how to improve our swing. Looking at the illustrations would help. A video would be useful. Having a golf pro demonstrate and talk us through the various parts of the swing would be even more useful. This person could answer our specific questions.

However, none of this learning will, by itself, improve our swing.

What we need is a second stage to the learning process. We must practise and get useful feedback. This involves hours on the driving range and putting greens. It involves spending money on more lessons.

The best sports people practise and train constantly. They know what they want to achieve and training is the process which gets them closer and closer to the levels of achievement they seek. All top international golf and tennis players today have personal coaches - people skilled in training and giving feedback.

Sport is not the only analogy. It is the same for any skill. Top musicians practise for hours each day. Mechanics working for racing teams are individuals who were willing to learn, practise and train to become the top exponents in their field.

Serious training and practice are not essential if we are prepared to play the game purely for enjoyment. However, our match results will mostly read as losses. This may not matter to the social golfer but in business it is a philosophy which does not stand well in the competitive markets of the twenty-first century.

Will you apply these winning processes and skills?

In this book we have provided the reader with a comprehensive look at the key skills necessary for the creation of high quality new clients. We have tried to be meticulous in the level of detail we have provided - not just stating what needs to be done but also giving illustrations of how it can be done. We have delineated the skills clearly.

The caveat is probably obvious. Reading this book and then doing no more will not result in anyone becoming a better seller. Training, practice and feedback will also be needed to translate the messages of this book into effective behaviour.

Obvious as this message may be, professionals are prone to overlooking it.

One reason is that they tend to be locked in by their own experience. For most professionals a great deal of their learning has come from reading books and listening to the pro. To develop the knowledge and understanding of the processes that underpin their profession this is a perfectly suitable method of learning.

Learning to use a skill is a different process.

Also, because professionals (rightly) value their time, this can translate into an unwillingness to devote time to new learning. We frequently receive requests to speak for an hour at a meeting or to run a brief after-hours training session.

The implicit assumption is that whilst it takes years to qualify as a top professional, one can learn to become a top business developer in the lunch hour! Professional salespeople who have spent their careers working to become more successful would find this concept laughable.

In this book we have sought to provide answers. We conclude with a question and a suggestion.

What will you do to incorporate all of the ideas, practices and skills contained in this book (which you do not apply today) in order for them to become 'normal' practice in your way of working?

The gap may be large - it may seem like attempting to eat an elephant. However, the solution to eating an elephant has been around for a long time. There is only one way to eat an elephant - bit by bit.

Pick a couple of ideas from this book that you believe will have immediate positive impact and begin application right away. Once these are working for you, take another and then another.

Choose small changes in behaviour that will lead to success. With success comes positive feelings and changed attitudes. With positive feelings and the right attitude the next step of implementation is so much easier and consequently more effective.

Just do something today!

Index